Beyond Healing:

The Path
To Personal Contentment
After Trauma

Dave Ziegler, Ph.D.

Executive Director,
Jasper Mountain,
Jasper, Oregon

ISBN 978-0-9814629-3-6
LCCN 2008927851

Published by Acacia Publishing, Inc.
Phoenix, Arizona
www.acaciapublishing.com

Printed and bound in the United States of America.

DEDICATION

In loving memory of my father, J. Guy Ziegler, 1922-2007. I hope to find some measure of the personal contentment he found in his life.

This volume is dedicated to each of you who have opened this book, particularly those of you who have experienced trauma in your life, those who have suffered the aftermath, and those who want more for yourself than what you see reflected in your mirror. I know how hard a climb life can be, but due to the trauma, you climb without shoes, with a heavy pack and with a physical disability or two. How do you manage? I have always admired the strength I see in each of you. What I want to say is how much stronger you are than others like me who have had it easier. My wish for you is that you could perceive your own strength and see how impressive it really is. You deserve to heal and you deserve happiness and personal contentment, and I hope this book can in some small way help guide you to what you so richly deserve.

Dave Ziegler

ACKNOWLEDGMENTS

An effort like this book requires many people to produce the final product. I want to thank some of these people. It has been such a great ride for me in my life—personally, socially and professionally. I have been able to learn from and work with so many wise and wonderful people.

This book is a bit of a departure for me. It is broader than my other works and allows me to bring in philosophical as well as psychological issues. It therefore includes ideas that come from many different people, some referenced and some not because the ideas came from within me but were put there by people I have admired and have learned from over the years.

In one of life's ironies, this book was written at a time of great stress in my professional life. My ideas and those of my organization, as well as our beliefs and approaches to helping others, were under attack, and this attack became personal towards me. The irony was after a day of bureaucratic regulators calling into question my decisions and even my integrity, I would sit down and continue writing about creating our own experience and moving toward personal contentment. I have had to repeatedly question whether anyone under these extreme and unfair conditions could be happy and at peace within, but that was exactly what I was writing about. I say this under acknowledgments because I want to thank the people who made this a difficult year and for making this project so very real through adversity. Mohandas Gandhi was unfairly imprisoned, was intentionally given a prison uniform filled with lice, and yet he thanked the guards responsible. His appreciation was honest because the guards helped him work on his anger and resentment. I have not been jailed, but in the same spirit I want to honestly thank those people who consider themselves adversaries of my program and of me. You helped me greatly by requiring me to live what I was writing. To do this, I had to struggle each day with creating a world I wished to live in while there were unfriendly pounding at my door.

I cannot forget to thank the many children, teens, and adults who have shared their trauma-filled lives with me and their difficult journeys to find a place of comfort, control, and meaning in their lives. Your journeys have all been inspiring to me and have taught me so much about resiliency.

We don't weather many storms without our support systems. I want to thank my wife, Joyce, my colleagues, and our organization's co-founder, Judy Littlebury. Thanks to all the hard-working staff of our agency, particularly Kiva Michels, Don Landauer, Dan Silver, and Jeff Huston. I also want to thank Debi Eisert for her support and hard work as the President of our organization's Board of Directors. Also, thanks to the other members of the Board: Chuck Davis, Linda Beach, Gary Buss, Steve Cole, Mike Kelly, Frank Papagni, Rob Morris, Gene Heinle, Randy Newalanic, Barb Lucas, Mike Kelly, Sharon Standfield and Parke Blundon.

I want to specifically thank the production team which helped me to reach the final product of a finished book: The Cricket Contrast for the cover and Karen Gray and her staff at Acacia Publishing. I want to thank John Ziegler and Judy Littlebury for their assistance and ideas.

I cannot fail to thank my parents, Guy and Rosemary, for building the foundation upon which my life has evolved. Your efforts to teach me and help others will live long after you are gone, and that is the biggest tribute that can be said of anyone.

TABLE OF CONTENTS

Dave Ziegler

INTRODUCTION

There is ample evidence that despite the challenges of modern living we have a greater potential than at any time in human history to be fulfilled and reach our dreams. However, just as in every era of human habitation on our planet, there is nothing easy about reaching our potential or living a full life filled with a deep sense of satisfaction. For some individuals the route to happiness and personal contentment is a path that is even more steep and difficult, and these are the people who have experienced significant traumatic experiences in life.

Although the points that are made in this book may apply to anyone, there is a particular target audience for these pages: people who have experienced trauma or are attempting to help someone who has a history of trauma. I believe it is important to state my premise early on and it is this: for all those who have taken the journey to heal the traumatic experiences of life, it is critical not to confuse the route with the destination; healing is not the destination, rather personal contentment and satisfaction with life is the real destination. Although the healing arts of psychiatry, psychology, medicine and others have made great strides to improve the lives of so many people, I believe we have fallen short of helping those on the healing journey reach their full potential. Too many times we set healing from trauma as the highest goal for traumatized individuals, but healing is only a stop along the route to personal contentment.

Although there is some evidence that human beings across cultures are predisposed to be happy (Diener &

Diener, 1995), it is clear happiness is not a universally achieved state of living. All the typically cited reasons why people do not live happy lives generally turn out to miss the mark as an explanation. Happiness has shown itself to be elusive, particularly in modern America. The promise of better health, longer lifespans, more technology, and instant access to information from around the world are now a reality for most of us, but have these advancements brought happiness with them?

If we consult the entertainment media, we find the formulas for happiness to be quite clear: the right aftershave, the right car, the right flat screen TV and a host of other consumer goods. Certainly all the great things we can purchase with our disposable income will enhance our sense of satisfaction, or will they? As we will see later on, the one thing that has not improved with all the factors that add to our quality of life is our personal contentment.

Those who look for reasons why happiness has eluded them will generally find ample reasons to explain their misfortune. But happiness is not beyond the reach of people with great stress in their lives, or those who are greatly challenged by careers, parenting, caring for elderly parents, financial struggles, or serious medical problems. It turns out that happiness has little to do with what is going on around us, but it has a great deal to do with what is going on inside of us.

I need to make an important point from the outset: this book will not rely on quick and catchy platitudes or easy formulas for achieving happiness. It will not suggest that you listen to the song *Don't Worry, Be Happy* multiple times per day. There is little that is easy in life. Our childhoods are often marked with confusion and a lack of power to impact what goes on around us. Adolescence is accompanied by greater pressure and expectations coming from all sides, and the need to figure out who we are and where we are going. Young adulthood brings both the fears as well as possibilities of making our own decisions and then being responsible for them on our own. Adulthood brings the pressures of family, career, child rearing and finding the limitations that life puts on our dreams. Midlife brings the growing stress of aging and recognizing the days ahead of us are fewer than those behind us. Old age brings the stark reality that no matter how difficult our life has been over the years, the final chapter is generally the most difficult in many respects: declining physical and psychological health, loneliness, the approaching winter of our lives, and the inevitable final chapter of the dying process. A number of observers of human existence have said something to the effect that "Living is not for wimps!"

The above description of the developmental periods of life may seem negatively skewed, but actually, for a very large segment of our population the realities of life are considerably more challenging than the description above. One of the quickest ways to have life go in a negative direction is to undergo some form of significant traumatic experience at any age in life. But the younger this happens, the more impactful it can be. These are the people for whom this book has been written, those who have had significant traumas in their lives either when young or later in life. This is a population segment that we have not fully assisted, in my opinion, to learn what it will take to reach their full potential. I believe that we have too often accepted something less than personal contentment in life when we only settle for the healing from abuse and trauma.

I want to make it clear that I feel a real urgency to communicate many of the things in this book. There is no time to lose. There is so much that we now know that gives us very good reasons to sit up and take notice regarding the decisions of living. I do not mean to blame anyone in these pages. I feel responsible for falling short myself. But being responsible is not blame, it is as the word implies: the ability to respond. As healing professionals and healing individuals, we must do more, we must do better, and the time is now.

So, if there is urgency to do something, what needs to be done? As I will explain in more detail in the following pages, traumatized individuals are paying an enormous and unacceptable price for the pain and trauma they have gone through. The urgency is to provide these individuals with the tools and support they need to move beyond the abuse and trauma they have experienced, and then to move beyond the healing process itself to reach levels of personal contentment in life. This is much more than a lofty-sounding ideal, it is quite literally a matter of life and death for this generation of survivors of traumatic experiences and for the generations that will come.

If we stop with healing past trauma and go no further, we risk throwing away our dreams and abandon the hope of living the uniquely satisfying life we all deserve to realize. We as a society also deprive ourselves of the potential contributions of a huge group of sensitive and creative individuals who can help make this a much better world. So, in a real sense the urgency is to stop waiting below the waterfall picking up the broken and battered bodies of all the people floating down the river and going over the falls. It is time to move upstream and fish people out of the dangerous pathways of physical, personal and spiritual death that we can now predict with increasing accuracy.

The urgency is compounded by the fact that traumatized individuals not only lose their own chance at psychological and physical health, resulting in widespread loss of human potential, but they model to their children the behavior of settling for less than life could bring them. This is one way the effects of trauma can be passed on from generation to generation.

When I say that we can predict some serious consequences, this is not an exaggeration. Significant trauma often does not heal without the right type of effective treatment. Because of the way the human brain processes and remembers serious trauma, the individual may become continually impacted by early events at each developmental stage of life. This can make all these stages of life not only considerably more negative, but also set the stage for dysfunction, disease, and an early death.

For people who struggle through life every day with isolation, anxiety and fear, the goal is not necessarily to prolong the lifespan when a poor quality of life exists. This would be similar to the Woody Allen joke that two older women are sitting in a greasy spoon restaurant and one says, "The food here is terrible," and the other adds, "Yes, and such small portions." Life is like this restaurant's food, we don't need larger portions of a bad thing. People need better, more fulfilled lives, not just longer ones. The real goal is to provide trauma survivors the healing they need and then take the next step to outline the path to reaching the potential they had before the trauma occurred in the first place. This is the path to personal contentment. It is not just about our own personal journey but also those we influence through modeling. Just as the modeling of negative coping styles teaches those lessons to our next generation, the person on the path to personal contentment models to our next generation the potential that life can offer.

If you think that my analogy of picking up the battered bodies at the bottom of the waterfall was a bit over the top, consider the following. America incarcerates more of its members than any society on the planet. We have greater proportions of our population in mental health, substance abuse, and psychiatric hospitals than any other country. We lag behind most of the industrialized world with our self-reports of life satisfaction. We also have the highest rates of child abuse for any nation for which we have data, thus ensuring a steady supply of traumatized individuals for the future. Over time, it is estimated that one third of our population falls below our own definition of individuals who are minimally functional in our society. I find it interesting that an estimated one third of our society also experienced significant traumatic experiences as children. The similarity of these two numbers, in my opinion, is not a coincidence.

The adage "An ounce of prevention is worth a pound of cure" is never more true than when trauma is considered. It is not a situation of, "pay me now or pay me later;" with trauma it is pay both now and later. My point is not only that trauma treatment is essential—that point has been adequately made over the last twenty years. I am saying that we must do more than heal from trauma. We must become resilient and continue on a path that cannot only make our life worth living, but can make a difference for others as well. I will accept that this may be a part of the spiritual healing from trauma—to return us to our deepest-held beliefs and goals. Is it beyond the realm of possibility that 10% of the traumatized individuals in our prisons or treatment programs could have instead become helpers for others to achieve healing and reach their own potential? I think not. By doing so, both the helper and the person helped come out ahead. But why stop with 10%? Many survivors of abuse and trauma have learned the value of helping others, and by doing so everyone heals and grows together.

These are the premises that will be explored in these pages. It is my intention to take a close, critical look at many of our beliefs about human limitations. Once our true potential is acknowledged, I believe the undeniable result is a message of hope. Hope for those individuals who have paid such a high price from past abuse and trauma, and hope for our future to reach our personal and collective human potential. If you are interested in such a journey but do not consider yourself to be someone who has endured significant trauma, then you might skim over the first three chapters. All of us have been bruised and even scarred by events in our lives. Even if you have not gone through major abuse in your life, the first three chapters may help you overcome lingering barriers to achieving your full potential that you may not even be aware of; we all have them.

We will start the journey by taking a close look at the importance of the healing process. We cannot go beyond healing until we have achieved healing. What do we need to heal from? When is this optional and when is it essential? How does the body adapt for healing or adapt for disease? Why does trauma present unique challenges to the healing process? What happens to untreated trauma? Are there similarities and differences in the way the individual heals the mind, the body and the spirit? These and other important issues of healing will be the subject of Chapter 1.

Chapter 2 attempts to show that healing has been the primary goal of all treatments related to trauma, but this has been both a part of the solution and part of the problem. Healing is not enough, although the treatment community has acted as if healing itself were enough. We have not set our sights high enough and the result is that we have insufficiently encouraged traumatized individuals to go beyond healing and achieve their goals.

This theme will continue into Chapter 3. No one wants someone who has been the victim of trauma to stay a victim. What about the ramifications of staying a survivor? If an individual gets stuck anywhere in life, this may very well limit the individual's personal growth. The treatment community at times has been so pleased with helping that we have encouraged those we have helped to wear the badge of "Survivor." We have even given this lofty title to the winner of a contest in one of our culture's most popular reality shows. For a time, it is appropriate to focus on being a survivor because it is an accomplishment to outlast abuse and life-threatening events. My message that this accomplishment is simply another potentially growth-producing opportunity on life's journey and should not define who the individual is. A significant and painful experience, yes, but a defining and limiting experience, no.

Chapter 4 takes a look at our happiness meter. As a culture, how are we handling the fact that we have more freedoms, more opportunities, more resources, and more access to pursue our interests than any culture in the history of the world? Has our great bounty brought us closer to happiness? One thing is clear; we can no longer claim ignorance of what makes people happy and unhappy. With a quick view at what we have done with our unprecedented good fortune, are we not plunging head first into the pursuit of unhappiness instead?

Life has never been easy, and although our modern world has certainly made a great deal of daily life easier than in the past, we continually develop new challenges that we must face and attempt to overcome. Just before writing this, I was listening to the national news, and it was pointing out that convicts on death row now have websites of their own. For example, you probably don't know this, but your young son or daughter can sign up to be a "special friend" of a notorious convicted murder on "MySpace." Why this is allowed is one issue, but the other issue is that the internet has brought with it new challenges that in many ways do not make life easier. Chapter 5 considers the ability of human beings to develop resiliency in the face of difficult times and even insurmountable odds.

Chapter 6 looks at the choices we all make and the power of these choices—not only choices of what we eat and how we act, but also how we think and choose to view ourselves, others, and the world around us. The point will be made that what we choose to do with our choices makes all the difference in the world. This is particularly true for traumatized individuals. How optimism produces very tangible differences in life in comparison to pessimism may surprise you.

Philosophers have discussed the esoteric connection of mind, body, and spirit since Plato. However, this subject has moved from the philosophy department to medical school. Chapter 7 will consider what we know about the influence of the mind/body connection. How the spirit comes into the mix will be covered in Chapter 9.

Chapter 8 will consider the importance of our connectedness with others and how social success is the building block of nearly every other type of success. If the goal is personal contentment in life, then social success is an essential ingredient.

The role of the spirit in the life of the individual is the topic of Chapter 9. We will see the history of the spirit as the basic foundation of mind and body, and then turning to the antithesis of mind and body in our recent past. This uneasy relationship of mind, body, and spirit with science is now coming back to an integrated understanding, which is outlined in the chapter.

At the risk of being another "how to" book, Chapter 10 provides some ideas for living. There will be very few surprises—we are beyond being surprised with our access to so much information. It is more a matter of setting goals, developing the skills, and then having the discipline to live a life that brings with it personal contentment. Anything short of personal contentment in life is a missed opportunity, and the people who most need to hear this are those who have been traumatized in life.

Throughout the book I will make some comments on issues going on in the culture around us. This is not due to my wandering mind. I am doing this intentionally because it is not possible to consider the topics of life satisfaction and happiness without looking at the influence of culture and the environment. Our culture gives us a perspective that influences our model of the world and how we feel about it. There is such a thing as an optimistic, stoic, fun-loving, and repressed culture. Our culture also has some specific influence on traumatized people. I will reflect on some of these issues in order for the reader to consider how we are all influenced, either to the positive or negative. If we become aware of how our society influences us then we have the choice to accept or change this influence. Feel free to disagree with any of my opinions, but I think you must agree that living right now in this culture is influencing each of us regarding our experience of life satisfaction, happiness and personal contentment.

Someone recently called me arrogant. At times I consult the dictionary to learn the background and a deeper meaning of words. Arrogant is from the Latin word to presume, and is used to mean making excessive claims or pretensions of superior importance or knowledge, such as pretending to know more than you do. Although not my intention, perhaps this book is arrogant in that it offers ideas about finding what each of us want most in life. Who am I to advise you, or anyone else on such an important topic? Those familiar with my other books know that I work with adults and children who have experienced significant trauma in their lives. I have been blessed with excellent training and experience and have nearly four decades of experience being a guide for people who are healing from trauma. To anyone wondering why they should be interested in my thoughts, I can only say that my journey has taught me a great deal, and I only wish to share some of what I have learned. I don't assume it will be of great value to you, and I hope that you do not find these pages pretentious or that I am overstating the case I make. But I will make a claim that is on a self-assurance to arrogance continuum, and that is that I know something about happiness and personal contentment. I live a life that has more of these qualities than anyone I know. You will find in these pages why I think I get such a huge return on my investment. I can assure you that I spend much more time being grateful for what I have than taking any credit for it.

So we have a long but interesting journey to take, and there is no time like the present to begin.

ONE

HEALING THE MIND, BODY, AND SPIRIT

The body has many methods to protect and heal itself. All these internal protections are designed to promote survival. For example, the body has upper limits of its pain threshold. When we reach these limits the nervous system can shut off and prevent the brain from allowing further pain stimuli to be acknowledged. This is referred to as shock, and can be a serious condition from which the organism may not recover. After all, the ability of the body to recognize pain is an important component of our internal survival mechanism. When the body can no longer handle the amount of pain being recorded by the brain, this is the equivalent of turning off the smoke detector due to too much heat—the result will likely not be positive.

The body has other shutdown systems designed to promote survival. Significant blood loss can lead to death, so how does anyone survive an accidental amputation? It turns out that when the body experiences an amputation, it protects itself by constricting the vascular system at the point of the injury to prevent serious blood loss.

There is an equivalent shutdown when the brain is overwhelmed with emotional pain. This off switch is referred to in psychology as dissociation, which is a frequent condition in cases of significant traumatic experience. Like its physical equivalent, dissociation creates problems at the same time it deadens the experience of psychological pain.

Trauma is one of the body's most challenging experiences. A working definition of trauma is any experience that overrides the ability of the individual to cope. The most impactful of traumas are those where the individual perceives a threat to survival and feels powerless to self-protect or effectively employ a last ditch crisis strategy of fight or flight. When this is understood, it is clear that some of the most damaging traumatic experiences occur to children, particularly young children, who have few methods to protect themselves.

While young children are particularly susceptible to traumatic experiences that have significant negative impact on the individual, sometimes for years after the trauma, it is also clear that everyone experiences some trauma in their lives. The loss of a pet or a loved one can leave us feeling powerless to prevent the emotional loss. Being fired from a desirable job, being left by a partner, or hearing that you have a serious medical illness can all result in some level of trauma. But all traumas are not the same, and the same external events may produce very different internal experiences. While we all experience traumas of some form, most traumas are not generally perceived as a threat to our very survival. But it is such a threat to survival that causes the most significant impact on the individual.

Trauma can be experienced very differently by different individuals. Because it is the experience of threat that can produce trauma, the seriousness of the event depends on the internal interpretation of how serious it is. For example, a perceived threat that may not be real can cause more trauma than an actual threat that is not recognized by the person. For this reason, it is important for all trauma therapists to learn how the person viewed their own experience and not to make assumptions based on how the therapist would have felt.

We also know that emotional injury can be helped when the individual expresses the feelings brought on by the emotional pain. The research of Pennebaker and others has demonstrated that the body has the ability to change its chemical structures based on processes such as psychotherapy (Pennebaker, Kiecolt-Glaser & Glaser, 1988). There is no question that the body is an amazing and efficient organism. At the same time, the body needs external help in order to heal.

❧❧

Jason had it all, and then it was gone

Some years ago I was asked to work with a young man who had a storybook childhood. He had two loving parents, a tight-knit family, many friends and great success in school. Jason was a natural athlete and excelled in most sports he tried. In high school he was the captain of the basketball team. His family often traveled to away games, and one winter, while doing so, the family car was involved in a terrible head-on collision. The car exploded and Jason's parents, brother and family dog were all immediately killed. In one second, his world changed forever. He not only lost his entire family, but he was sent to live with relatives in another state, resulting in the loss of his home, his school, all his friends and the life that he knew. This healthy, outgoing young man turned sullen and dark for years after this experience. He was able to fight back and regain some of who he was inside himself, but the life he had would never be recoverable. Jason will struggle with this trauma for the rest of his life, but with years of psychological help he has battled back from the experience to a very impressive degree.

᳔᳔᳔

Because we are all wounded in some way or another, trauma appears to be a challenging aspect of the human experience. It even appears that nature realizes this and can respond in ways to promote survival and perhaps even promote thriving as a result of the stress of trauma. Understanding the capacity of the brain to be resilient to traumatic experience—in other words, the ability to bounce back from adversity—is an important component of trauma treatment and recovery.

We have mentioned the body's ability to respond to overwhelming physical pain through a process of shutting down pain receptors in the brain. We have also mentioned the psychological equivalent where the brain shuts down incoming emotional pain receptors through dissociation. But the brain has another important ability, which is to integrate past experiences in a way that adapts the brain to prepare for future experiences in a successful way.

A general rule of trauma therapy is that what has caused the problem can also promote the solution. I am not talking about the cause being the traumatic event itself, but the meaning of the event to the individual's brain. For example, extreme athletes perform tasks that would traumatize a normal individual—jumping off a cliff with a parachute, swimming with sharks, or the many new and more death defying stunts being tried these days. My brother recently retired as a career pilot for a major airline. I'm sure that he would not consider himself a risk junkie, but he volunteered and was given the task of flying to 40,000 feet in a new commercial jetliner and shutting down all the engines. He was to see how the plane responded while he attempted to restart the plane's engines in flight. I get nervous writing about this, but it was all in a day's work for him. I would assume he had a few exciting moments with this project, but for him it was a positive and exciting challenge, not the life threatening experience it would have been for me.

With repetition the brain begins to perceive, rightly or wrongly, that the individual has the ability to influence the outcome of a stressful and even highly threatening event. The brain may block alarm signals to avoid threatening situations at its own peril. It is the internal meaning of the threat that can be changed to make the individual stronger rather than weaker.

In general, the brain responds to a traumatic experience by making the alarm center of the brain—the limbic system and the amygdala in particular—sensitized to any incoming stimulus that reminds the brain of past trauma. This is the source of most of the long-term negative impacts of traumatic experiences. However, with a few adjustments in the way the body physiologically responds to significant stress, the body learns to incorporate stress into a positive adaptation which can strengthen rather than damage the individual. To better explain this, we need to consider the way the mind/body heals.

The Healing Process

This chapter will not be a full treatment of the healing of trauma. For this, I refer the reader to the book *Traumatic Experience and the Brain* (Ziegler, 2002). However, if we are to consider why it is important not to stop with healing, it seems essential that achieving some measure of healing must be our first step.

Although the body has a variety of ways to promote survival and overall health, at times some of the methods it employs can bring about the opposite results. Trauma is a very good case in point. Because traumatic experience by definition is understood by the body as a threat to the very survival of the individual, the brain has critically important methods of responding to such trauma. Much like the process of physical shock, which protects the body from pain but also makes the body vulnerable to system failure, the brain's significant response to trauma can produce temporarily positive results, but long-lasting problems as well.

Since trauma is perceived by the brain as a threat to survival, it responds in an all-out crisis mode. Normal functioning is displaced by an immediate and complete system response to the threat. This can be called the stress response cycle. In this response the brain activates a complex system of glands, hormones, and neurotransmitters for the purpose of responding as effectively as possible to the perceived threat.

Figure 1: The Stress Response Cycle

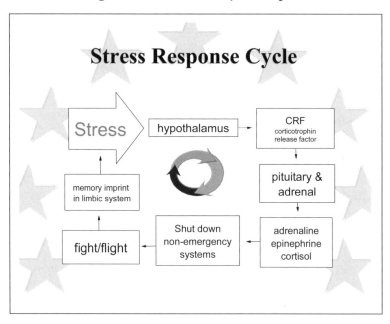

Figure 1 depicts the stress response cycle. Although the brain and arousal system of any healthy human being is going to have a stress reaction that can be explained in this diagram, traumatized individuals have the most to lose from this pattern of responding to stress. This is because the center of the brain, the limbic system, sets off this stress cycle more often if the individual has experienced significant trauma in the past. This cycle can produce a habitual response to major or minor stress that can bring a host of psychological and even physical problems that we will soon see.

Stress is inherent to living. In fact, one measure of signs of life is the ability to detect some stress responses in brain activity. Stress is all around us, and most of the time we learn to live with it. After a significant traumatic experience, the brain's ability to work effectively with stress can be seriously compromised. Stress is detected by the hypothalamus in the brain. The hypothalamus has the function of preparing the organism to respond as needed to survive the threat that has caused the stress. The way the hypothalamus does this is to produce a chemical called a cortical release factor or CRF that stimulates the pituitary (the body's master gland) and the adrenal glands. The stimulated glands release hormones such as adrenaline, epinephrine and cortisol. The purpose of this system-wide release of hormones and neuro-transmitters is to prepare the body for a fight or flight response to the threat causing the stress.

The chemical signals that race through the body in a blink of an eye send the message that unless immediate action is taken, survival is threatened. To the body, a threat to survival is the most serious signal received by the brain, and it will always take precedence over any other signals being received. For example, the sex drive is one of the brain's strongest drives and aids in the survival of the species. However, when a mountain climber nearly falls and is holding onto a ledge for dear life, the odds are very good that thoughts of survival are taking immediate precedence over any sexual thoughts. The fight-or-flight response involves chemical signals throughout the body to shut down all non-essential functions and send immediate energy to the areas of the body needed to handle the threat. Essential parts of the body, for example the large muscle groups in the legs and arms, receive additional blood, oxygen, and adrenaline. At the same time, blood rushes to the brain's sensory receptors, making the individual hypersensitive to his/her surroundings.

When the stress response cycle is initiated, and the result is a significant traumatic experience, meaning the response of the body has not prevented nor adequately addressed the threat, this experience is coded as a traumatic memory in the limbic system. This form of memory is designed to help the individual by being an intense reminder of a traumatic event so anything similar can be avoided in the future. However, this cycle can hinder as well as help by making the brain more hypersensitive to reminders of the stress that caused the traumatic experience, and over time, to any related stress or any stress at all. This pattern can develop into an ongoing cycle of stress and overreaction causing the fight-or-flight response, and the experience of powerlessness over the threat and the stress being stored in the limbic memory.

While the release of hormones, such as cortisol, are helpful in responding to a real crisis (fighting off an attacker or running for help, for example), sustained release of cortisol in the body damages cells, particularly neurons. Continued release of cortisol begins to break down the cells of the body, which can produce a wide range of emotional or psychological damage initially and, over time, can produce significant physical damage.

The goal of the stress response cycle, as seen in the above explanation, is two-fold. First, the body is prepared to meet the present threat with a survival response of fight or flight. Second, the traumatic memory function of the brain's limbic system stores the information of the experience and adds it to the internal memory of situations and events that the brain wants to avoid in the future. However, both of these goals can be problematic at times. For example, fight or flight may not be of much use to the young child who experiences a situation beyond his or her control or ability to respond with effectiveness. In such cases, the most typical response of the brain is to institute a type of flight known as psychic numbing or dissociation. In these cases the individual is taken away from the stress emotionally and psychologically due to the inability of the body to flee physically. However, this is not sufficiently effective to actually protect the body either physically or psychologically, and further ramifications are likely for the individual.

The second goal of preserving a traumatic memory to avoid similar situations can also be problematic for the individual. If a child has an unfortunate run-in with the family cat who did not appreciate having its tail pulled while it was eating dinner, the angry response of the cat along with the pain of the scratches may help the child avoid a similar painful situation in the future. However, traumatic memories are not always specific in a way that is helpful to the individual. For example, the traumatic memory of the angry cat and the slashing claws to a young child may generalize to all cats in all situations or even all animals in all situations. When it comes to traumatic memories, the brain always errs on the side of false positives, or if in doubt, sounds the alarm from past traumatic experiences. When this takes place, it may be the start of a serious and eventually catastrophic series of events.

The problem with the brain's response to perceived trauma is that it can and often does overdo the protective response. The brain may overstate the threat faced by the individual and over-respond to the situation. In fact, the short and long-term consequences of trauma come down to just this issue. The seriousness of the initial threat to the survival of the individual causes the brain to overreact to future threats. This is even more likely with children than it is with adults. Because trauma is a function of the internal experience as a response to the nature of the external threat, children are least equipped with the experience and understanding necessary to fully assess the level of threat being faced in an accurate way. After a significant trauma, young children may internally experience such an intense threat to survival that they continue to perceive, and thus experience, the event repeatedly, like a flashback that doesn't seem to end.

The alarm response and even the fight-or-flight mechanism of the autonomic nervous system are designed to aid survival and avoidance of threat. However, with some individuals, the internal alarm response and the initiation of the fight-or-flight sequence of hormones and neurotransmitters actually becomes more of a threat to the individual than any external threat.

When an individual is caught in the continual cycle of experiencing and reacting to stress that is perceived as more threatening than it actually is, this can produce mental illness or dis-ease within the mind/body of the individual. Some names for this are posttraumatic stress disorder, and various forms of depression, anxiety disorder, panic attacks, phobias, or agoraphobia, which is becoming so overwhelmed with panic that the individual cannot leave his/her home. As bad as these problems are, if this negative cycle of stress continues it ceases to be helpful to the individual, and it can cause major breakdowns of the body's physical systems resulting in physical disease and even premature death. Research findings on these potential results will be discussed later in this chapter.

The Short-term and Long-term Effects of Traumatic Experience

The consequences of untreated traumatic experience can be daunting. The physical and emotional pain of the experience is only the beginning. The initial trauma can cause immediate negative consequences, new difficulties as the individual matures, poor social success resulting in lack of support and isolation, and then end in emotional or even physical breakdown and premature death. If this sounds as if the consequences of untreated traumatic experiences are being exaggerated, consider the following.

Since we all face life experiences that can override our ability to physically and emotionally cope with a situation, some trauma is a part of the human experience. In the following description of the negative results of untreated trauma, we are considering significant traumatic experiences that led the individual to view the situation as life-threatening and the individual's brain to remember the experience as a threat to survival. Even with this level of trauma, it has been estimated that as many as 4 million children are exposed to such trauma every year in the United States (Perry, 1994). The results of such serious trauma can include short-term and long-term consequences.

Short-term consequences of significant traumatic experiences such as serious child abuse include the following:

- Immediate psychological and/or physical pain.
- Loss of trust in those whom the child needs for protection and support.
- Hypervigilance toward persons, places or things that the child associates with the traumatic experience.
- Loss of self-regulation, such as crying, raging, excessive fear, and associated behavioral outbursts.

- Loss of the opportunity to be a child, such as the loss of the ability to play, to learn, to enjoy, to laugh, due to being concerned that the experience has not ended.
- Loss of the ability to feel pleasure and contentment.
- High levels of distraction, defensiveness and hostility.
- Poor attention span.
- Sleep disturbances.
- Higher statistical chance of further trauma.
- Self-directed aggression.
- Dissociation and psychic numbing.
- Over-activation to trauma, deprivation in other areas of life.
- Impaired attachment.
- Pervasive negativity.
- Negative impact on executive functions.
- Stress response cycle activated by minor situations.
- Poor social and relational skills.
- Becoming emotionally stuck at the level at which the trauma occurred.

Long-term consequences build on these negative effects on the individual due to the brain remembering the events in a special way so as to be prepared to avoid any possible repetition of the traumatic event. These longer-term issues can include the following:

- Damage to physical and psychological health over time.
- Misinterpreting social and environmental cues leading to poor social success.
- High levels of fear and anxiety.
- Personal isolation.
- Organizing one's life around negative experiences.
- Consistent reactive emotions and behaviors.
- Personal powerlessness, which can result in negative traits, such as a controlling manner.
- Being distant from others needed for personal support.

- Affective blindness and not seeing the needs of others.
- Becoming stuck in negative coping styles.
- Inability to use feelings as guides for decisions and behavioral responses.
- Personal emptiness.
- Developing risk behaviors, such as addictions that compensate for inner emptiness.
- The experience of reliving the trauma.
- Self-harm and suicidality.
- Poor work/career performance.
- Negative views of self, others, life.

A close look at the above list can show that initial reactivity to a traumatic experience can become habitual and lead to more serious negative coping styles over time. For this reason, traumatic experience can become more negatively impactful on the individual in future years. However, there is more bad news concerning untreated trauma, which can best be explained by the following medical research.

The Adverse Childhood Experience Study

Thousands of medical research studies are conducted and published each year. Occasionally there is a study that has surprising results that point to making major changes in the way we think about a topic of health. Just such a study, or more correctly a series of studies, has been published by the Center for Disease Control and Kaiser Permanente's Department of Preventive Medicine. The principal researcher, Dr. Vincent Felitti, describes the surprising findings of the research as nothing short of calling for a change in the way we provide medical care in this country. This series of studies researched the underlying causes of the ten most common causes of death in America. The results have surprised basically everyone in the medical community, including the researchers themselves. The research identified the primary cause of the top ten physical illnesses leading to premature death as adverse childhood experiences, which are most often some form of child abuse. The result of the research produced its name, which is referred to as the Adverse Childhood Experiences Study (Felitti, Anda, Nordenberg, Williamson, Spitz, Edwards, Koss, 1998).

Doctor Felitti explains that the study produced a result that was a complete surprise to him. He is a medical doctor with a background in internal medicine. Before this research he knew little about child abuse or how early traumatic experiences had any impact on the health of adult populations. Some of the key findings of the research are:

- Adverse childhood experiences, often child abuse, are the primary cause of disease and serious medical problems in later life, including the ten leading causes of premature death in the United States.
- Physical disease later in life is often emotionally based
- Early adverse experiences can result in physical disease later in life.
- Disturbed neurological patterns develop as a result of adverse experiences, adding to the development of physical disease.
- Early adverse experiences are the main determinant of the health and social well-being of the nation.
- The research points to a needed shift in the way pediatric and adult medical care are provided.

I am a frequent critic of research because I believe many published research studies do not satisfy basic requirements of scientific inquiry. To be scientific a study must be objective, must attempt to disprove a hypothesis, and must have a research design that does not promote a desired finding. When I shine the light of scientific inquiry on the ACE Study, it meets the test. Although there is no such thing as perfect research, the ACE Study was conducted in the correct way—large sample, objective researchers with no desired result that was predetermined, a solid research design, the results came from the data, and the unanticipated findings were reported.

As revolutionary as these findings are, there is a point that is even more impactful—this study has not been recently released, it has been published in dozens of medical journals for nearly ten years. The fact that we now know that early traumatic experiences eventually develop into organic physical disease leads to the question, "What have we done with this critical information?" The answer, Dr. Felitti is quick to respond, is "very little." Some of the least interested professionals in the findings of this research are medical doctors, who are precisely the audience the researchers had hoped to reach. With the frequency of published articles over the years, it appears that the medical profession has indeed taken some notice, but the response has been underwhelming to say the least.

I mention this research for several reasons. The study clearly supports the mind/body connection. It identifies some of the most ominous outcomes of untreated traumatic experience. It also points to the fact that our nation's medical, psychiatric and mental health systems are insufficiently responding to the need for change when it comes to delivering services. Kaiser Permanente has offered one possible way medical services could be changed. This large Heath Maintenance Organization has started to treat the causes of disease (early traumatic experience) as well as the medical symptoms that are presented in the clinics. The results of this change have been positive, with better outcomes including fewer clinic visits for those receiving psychological treatment for traumatic experiences. The bottom line for the HMO is to save money while providing better patient care.

But why have the rest of the nation's healthcare providers ignored this research? The answer is unknown other than to wonder if the bureaucratic status quo within the healthcare industry is too powerful to acknowledge any voice for change—even if the result may be better patient outcomes and ultimately lower healthcare costs.

How We Heal From Traumatic Experience

We don't heal from trauma until the conditions that brought about the trauma are no longer a threat to us. This does not just mean that the threat is gone, it means that the individual must experience that the threat is gone, and this can be a very different thing. For children, trauma is experienced as never-ending. Particularly for young children, their sense of time is subjective. When they are having fun, time goes very quickly, when they need to wait for something, time crawls by at an intolerably slow pace.

After a serious trauma occurs, and particularly if it occurs more than once, the child is waiting, or more specifically, the child's limbic system is waiting, for the threat to reappear. Since the brain's fear center, the amygdala, sounds the alarm in response to any related stress, the child experiences that the trauma has returned. This can also be true for adolescents and even adults. The emotional developmental level of the traumatized individual is often arrested at the age that the trauma first occurred. This means that for many traumatized teens and adults, their emotional level may be stuck in childhood years. Healing cannot begin until the individual is safe and experiences the safety that includes the absence of any threat that reminds the individual of the initial trauma.

ॐ✑

For Tera, everything adults wanted was a threat

*For many victims of the trauma of sexual abuse,
the brain becomes hypersensitive to the desires of
others. Tera was only seven, but her seven year old
brain had faced the sexual desires of two adult males in
her life. The outward symptom coming from her past
was intense non-compliance with all adults. When an
adult wanted something from her, she did the opposite.
In Tera's case, her brain's fear center set off an
indiscriminate alarm whenever it picked up any desire
from an adult, sexual or not. For Tera to get beyond
protecting herself with oppositional behavior, we had to
change the way she perceived the desires of adults. We
eventually did this, but it was a slow process.*

๛

Trauma does not get better with time, and it does not
heal from distancing oneself from memories of one's
traumatic past. To just stop thinking about it does not work
for a very specific reason. The limbic system of the brain
does not need the explicit or factual memory to think about
the trauma; the traumatic memories in the limbic system
handle this function. The difference in the two is that the
individual has some control over explicit memories, while
implicit memories in the limbic system are not under
conscious control. This can make a big difference. The more
the individual can begin to experience some control over
trauma memories, the sooner healing is possible.

Traumatic memories of events that go beyond the
person's ability to cope are not the real problem. We can all
remember events in our lives that we wish did not happen.
But unless these memories carry with them the baggage of
emotional reactivity, they are just unpleasant memories.

The problem with traumatic memories is how they carry harmful affective and physical responses from past events. We begin to heal as we learn how to turn off the stress response cycle and remember the past as an unpleasant memory, not one that carries significant emotional content and stress.

There are a variety of ways that we can learn to turn down the volume on our internal reactivity brought on by stress. All healthy people have learned ways to lighten their load, find enjoyable pursuits and, at least for a time, relax and enjoy the moment. For many people this is called a weekend. The pressures and stress of the work week will all be back soon enough, but for some precious hours we turn it off through recreation and activities that have the ability to recharge our batteries. The healthiest people don't wait for a weekend because they have learned immediate ways to turn off or de-condition harmful internal reactivity.

Once we can remember our traumatic past and learn to turn off the emotional reactions to a large or small degree, we can begin to put the past in perspective. It happened, it was painful, it was unfortunate, and it is over. At times, the brain needs to hear a continual message that the traumatic experience is over. It helps when memories trigger emotional reactions and the individual can hit the off button of the internal response. This goes a long way to conveying the message to the fear center of the brain that the trauma is in the past and not in the present or around the next corner.

Chronic perceptions of feeling unsafe or still at risk usually result in some form of dysfunctional behavior. It may be to fight or run from a situation where neither response is helpful. It may be to reach for the anesthesia that always works, at least in the short run, such as drugs, alcohol, food, nicotine, sex, gambling or other addictions. Therefore, the next step to healing is to gain internal control over our behavioral reactions to trauma. These behaviors run the continuum from isolation and solitary inactivity, to frantic and even high-risk behavior that is meant to distract the individual from the ever-present fear for one's life. When we learn to think more clearly about our traumatic past and learn to de-condition harmful emotional reactivity, we can then learn more positive adaptive behaviors that help us rather than make our lives more difficult.

When we are able to get our negative thoughts about the past, our incapacitating emotions, and our maladaptive behaviors all behind us, we have a much better chance to engage life in fulfilling ways. This can lead to a positive spiral in the same way trauma can lead to a negative spiral. When we successfully engage life, several things usually happen. We begin to like ourselves, we run into people who find us more enjoyable, and we begin to feel that others enjoy us. Each of our successes helps us to build a more positive internal view of ourselves and our world.

But not all traumas can be relegated to the past. There will always be more stress in life and perhaps more traumatic experiences both small and large. When new stresses come up, we must learn to be skillful at using real-time strategies to prevent further traumatizing events. The best way to do this is to develop coping styles sufficient to keep life's challenges from overwhelming us. The more we practice our new and more successful coping styles, the more we insulate ourselves from the traumatic events in life. We cannot avoid the many stresses that come to everyone, but we can keep the stresses from becoming bigger than our ability to handle them.

I have taken the above trauma healing process and broken it down to the ten steps of treating traumatic experience. The ten steps are:

1. Establish safety, trust, and exploration.
2. Explore how trauma is perceived, experienced, and acted upon.
3. Explore trauma memories.

4. De-condition harmful affective responses.
5. Re-exposure to the trauma.
6. Cognitively restructure the meaning of the trauma.
7. Replace problematic behaviors with adaptive behaviors.
8. Build a new internal self-perception.
9. Learn coping strategies.
10. Practice self-mastery.

These ten steps are a guide to the process of overcoming the harmful effects of trauma. A lengthy discussion of these steps can be found in *Achieving Success With Impossible Children* (Ziegler, 2005).

Why So Many People Never Achieve Healing

Evidence suggests the aftereffects of trauma can be very devastating to the individual and can literally change the quality and length of the person's life. The evidence further suggests that the right type of help can make a big difference in heading off many of the long-term negative results of trauma. Knowing this, why would anyone choose to avoid help and, in so doing, essentially sentence oneself to a life of pain and isolation? There may be several answers to this question that, when recognized, may help to avoid or overcome the obstacles to necessary healing. Before considering these obstacles, there are a couple of exceptions to note.

First, it has already been stated that trauma is an aspect of the human experience and to one degree or another touches everyone. But in the same way that not all soldiers coming home from war suffer Posttraumatic Stress Disorder, not all trauma victims develop significant life-changing reactions. This may be because of the support around the person, it may be because the person has a natural tendency to self-heal, or it may be because the individual has the ability to internally change the external experience. An example of this last point is the wartime experience of my father.

ॐॐ

Not trauma, but triumph

As a young man of twenty-four, my father was asked by his country to routinely risk his life flying his B-26 over enemy territory. His plane was hit by ground fire numerous time, he lost crew members, he witnessed friends being shot down, then was asked to get some rest and do it all again the next day. My father had every right to develop traumatic stress from this extended experience for years during WW II, but he did not. His perception of this experience appears to explain this result. After all, he was being asked by his country to save the world from an evil dictator. He had the support of his fellow soldiers, of a grateful country and of the free world. There was meaning and purpose in this risky undertaking, and in his mind the risk was more than worth taking. Not only did this ongoing traumatic experience not adversely affect my father's subsequent life, it became the focus of a book he wrote, a social network that he enjoyed, an internal meaning of the glorious victory of right over wrong that he was proud to be a part of and, thus, the highlight of his life.

ॐॐ

The second point is that the best way to know if trauma has adversely affected you is to take a close look to see if the experience has affected your ability to experience life to its fullest. I would offer two principles in this regard. If a child has been traumatized, I would provide treatment until it was not further indicated. For children, it appears the safest course is to act with preventive concern. Children often cannot tell you of internal changes in their view of self or others, or may not have fully formed a solidified understanding of the world around them to notice that it has changed due to trauma. Therefore, for children some level of trauma treatment is recommended. For an adult, I would only suggest treatment if it were indicated based on negative impacts on daily living. This would not preclude a "check up" by a professional to help the individual identify potential trauma impacts. At times, traumatized people do not notice rather startling internal impacts of trauma and may gain insight into these issues with help in self-reflection.

But the reality is that many adults and children do not get the help they need, when they need it. This often results in tragedy that could have been avoided. One of the obstacles to getting the right kind of timely help is believing that the negative results of traumatic experience will gradually get better over time. Just like the story of the frog sitting in the water as the water gradually heats up, and not noticing until it is too late, traumatic experience can cause internal changes that gradually become accepted and become the status quo. One example of this was a minister client of mine who was surprised that I expressed concern over his use of Valium as a social lubricant. He did not see it as a problem that he took medication to get in front of his congregation or that he took his pills before meeting with a parishioner. In fact, he was taking Valium every day and sometimes multiple times per day just to give him "confidence" to do his job. His traumatic past was seriously affecting his daily functioning in his life's work, and he did not, or perhaps would not, acknowledge to himself what was plain to see.

We are all reinforced by life experience with the belief that the aftermath of traumatic experiences will go away or get better with time. We have watched as illnesses get better with time, disappointments get better, feelings of sadness, grief and loss almost always get better — why not the results of trauma? Unfortunately, gradual improvement may not be the outcome of significant traumatic experience. Over time, we all seem to be capable of making significant alterations that soon become our internal status quo or what we consider normal, such as a minister being unable to face his congregation without taking medication for anxiety.

Like other illnesses of either the body or mind, many people prefer to underestimate the problem or the seriousness of the condition. Doctors talk of emphysema patients who smoke two packs a day, diabetics who do not follow their diet, and patients with high blood pressure who refuse to take lifesaving medication. In fact, physicians will tell you that the number one frustration of doctors (not counting insurance companies) is not an inability to diagnose the problem, but an ability to get the patient to cooperate in a regimen that will promote health. If many of us prefer to ignore physical illness, how much easier is it to ignore psychological distress that we believe others are not aware of? Like the above examples of physical illness, the results of ignoring the adverse consequences of trauma can be very detrimental in the short and long run.

The last reason many people do not ask for help with the psychological consequences of traumatic experience is their need to convince themselves that they are not really sick, or that they are not "crazy" and do not need a shrink. Many of us go to great lengths to try to convince ourselves that we are not ill enough to go to the doctor. We are not an alcoholic just because we drink to get through every day, and bad things happen to everyone so why talk about it? But the truth is that at some point we become ill enough to get help; the negative coping styles have, for example, developed into chemical dependency, and the bad things that have happened to us will affect our ability to fully live our lives without the help we need.

How Do We Spiritually Heal?

Physical and psychological healing have been discussed, but what about healing the spirit? As we will see in Chapter 9, the importance of spiritual healing in reaching satisfaction in life is fundamental. Medicine and psychology have acknowledged the role the spirit plays in overall health, and they no longer ignore or show antagonism toward spiritual healing. By the word "spiritual" I mean the most fundamental and deepest core beliefs of the individual that guide, support, and inform each of us. At times we hear that someone lost his or her "moral compass," which means the individual began to ignore the guidance of the conscience to make decisions that align with core beliefs. When this happens, there can be an impact not only on the spirit of the person but on the mind and body as well.

The spirit can be damaged by many things. We can lose our spiritual bearings by consistent choices that violate our internal principles. We can lose hope in the face of overwhelming loss or discouragement. We can lose the first step in the "golden rule" (treat others as you would have them treat you), which is to believe that we deserve to be treated with respect and consideration. We can lose heart and believe that our mistakes are beyond forgiveness. We can also isolate ourselves from our own internal spring of love, from the support of others, and distance ourselves from our higher power, God, or our connection with nature around us.

Spiritual health could be defined as living in harmony with our inner core beliefs and principles. It is not uncommon for the spiritual health of an individual to be adversely affected by physical or psychological dis-ease. It is also not uncommon for spiritual illness to be manifested as well in physical or psychological illness. Regardless of where disease begins, the healing process is most successful when healing steps are taken in all three areas simultaneously.

The process of achieving spiritual health is to do an internal assessment and recommit to a return to one's inner beliefs and principles. If facing physical problems is problematic to some people, taking an honest appraisal of one's life in relation to inner beliefs can be even more frightening and difficult. Many people prefer to keep their beliefs to themselves, while others prefer to surround themselves with a community of like-minded individuals who reflect the individual's values. For example, some look at the Amish people and wonder how hard it is to live a life of intentional austerity. However, many Amish look at the "English" as sad and isolated people who are controlled by technology and frantically search for meaning they do not find in their modern world. Which is true? It just depends on the view from your vantage point. The deep faith and resiliency of the Amish beliefs and social network impressed the world when a gunman senselessly killed five Amish children in a school in Pennsylvania and then killed himself. In response, the Amish community grieved in their traditional way, immediately forgave the murderer and sent moral and financial support to the family of the deranged murderer. While the Amish mothers and fathers loved their children every bit as much as non-Amish parents, it is only the strength of their inner beliefs and principles that allowed forgiveness and the strength to face another day after such an overwhelming tragedy.

In the last chapter forgiveness will be one of the suggested approaches to enhance personal contentment. From a psychological point of view it is important to mention what forgiveness is and is not. Forgiveness is not pardoning, excusing, condoning, denying, forgetting or reconciliation with the person forgiven (McCullough, Pargament & Thoresen, 2000). Forgiveness is a choice to alter one's position about a perceived offense and often involves a better understanding of the person who committed the perceived offense (Harris, Thoresen & Lopez, 2007). Forgiveness will be a suggested strategy because it has been found to help eliminate the many negative influences of being stuck in anger, resentment or carrying a grudge (Harris & Thoresen, 2005; Thoresen, Harris & Luskin, 2000; McEwen, 1998).

Every major belief system has principles to live by. All have a basic formula that dis-ease comes from separation and health comes from harmony and connectedness. This includes connection with God, with Yahweh, Jehovah, Allah, Shiva, Atman, the Great Spirit, the Tao, Christ consciousness or other sources of spiritual power. Connection also includes the family of man, the fellow believers, community, or satsang. For spiritual health to be alive and well we must be in harmony and connection with the source of our spiritual strength and connected with something greater than ourselves.

When such a connection is broken, the job is to reconnect. Once again, each spiritual system has a map for reconnection, such as prayer, meditation, contrition, atonement, or ritualized observance. For others, spiritual reconnection can take place through self-reflection, a quiet retreat, a recommitment to self and values such as in a twelve step program or other paths to realign internal priorities. Regardless of our beliefs or involvement or lack of involvement in an organized spiritual belief system, we all are obligated to follow our moral compass or we become estranged from our beliefs, ourselves and others. Spiritual dis-ease can result in physical and/or psychological illness due to the mind/body/spirit connection.

The Balance of Health

But just as there are pressures that pull us from health such as those mentioned above, there are also natural tendencies that move toward health. I cannot cite research for this, but I have noticed that when a person achieves a measure of health in one area, there is a positive tension toward health in other areas of the person. For example, when someone makes a personal commitment to lose weight, exercise and eat right, as this process brings health to the physical body, there is often a desire or drive to improve upon health in other areas. Consider the athlete who develops a world class body and feels a drive to improve his or her mind, or highly evolved intellectuals who feel a need to improve on their spiritual health.

This appears to me to be a type of balance and unfortunately it appears to work both ways. While there is a type of internal pressure to move toward health, there can also be a system-wide move in the direction of unhealthy choices. Both of these processes appear to be cyclical in nature. This brings up the need to keep the body, mind and spirit moving in unison in a positive direction toward health.

Healing Is the First Order of Business, but not the Last Step

Healing from significant traumatic experience can be, in the short or long term, a matter of life and death as well as a matter of the quality of life that the individual lives. The healing stage following a traumatic experience is critically important for the individual. But the premise of this book is that, in part because this process is so poorly understood or so infrequently accomplished successfully, traumatized individuals are not encouraged to go beyond the healing process. Encouraging those who have been traumatized to take the path to personal contentment is the goal of the following chapters.

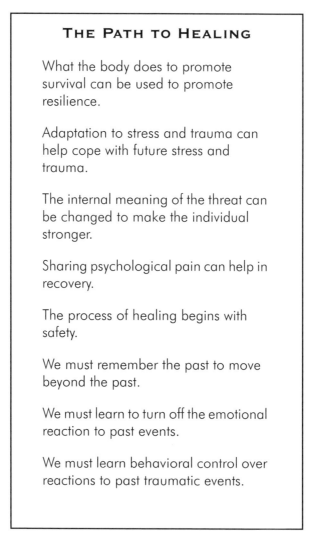

THE PATH TO HEALING

What the body does to promote survival can be used to promote resilience.

Adaptation to stress and trauma can help cope with future stress and trauma.

The internal meaning of the threat can be changed to make the individual stronger.

Sharing psychological pain can help in recovery.

The process of healing begins with safety.

We must remember the past to move beyond the past.

We must learn to turn off the emotional reaction to past events.

We must learn behavioral control over reactions to past traumatic events.

Two

Healing Has Never Been Enough

More than two decades ago, a foster child came into my family who had been in the process of healing from child abuse for some time. I was informed when she arrived that her caseworker wanted her to continue her involvement in a special treatment group for children who had been sexually victimized. That sounded to me like a very good idea until I inquired how long she had been a member of this specific treatment group. The answer came back that over the previous three years the group had been a weekly activity for the ten-year-old young lady. With obvious pride the caseworker told me that the young lady, "really likes the group and most of her closest friends are in the group." The caseworker said that she was sure that I would want her to continue this very important "treatment."

The caseworker was wrong; I was moderately horrified. It was not that I disagreed with getting treatment for a sexually abused child, nor did I disagree with the idea of group therapy for children in this situation, something I endorse wholeheartedly. However, there were several problems here. She had memorized the language of the group, "my body is my own…it was not my fault…no one has the right to invade my space…" She had learned the disclosure story and could recite it to anyone interested, "I was sexually touched by my stepfather and my grandpa and…" After several years of telling her story, it had long since lost its emotional connection within the young lady. It was as if she were once again saying what she did on her summer vacation. It reminded me of what some therapists who work with alcoholics called the "alcolog," or a story told so often it had become nearly a recorded tape and with little emotional connection and limited value. However, none of this was the primary problem. What I objected to was the fact that while no one seemed to notice, this young lady had spent nearly one third of her life, and some very important formative years, hearing how she was first a victim and now a survivor of sexual abuse. This ingrained storyline was the highlight of her week, when she and all her friends, also survivors of sexual abuse, got together and were praised and reinforced for being so strong that they could face their abuse and be a member of this club.

I did not immediately stop her involvement, but I did attend the next two groups. What I saw led me to challenge both the caseworker and the therapists running the group. Everyone thought that this was a great experience for abused children and I agreed. But it was not an indefinite great experience for every child. Did they notice that the strongest aspect of this child's identity, social network and support system all revolved around her being defined as someone who had been sexually abused, and who was busy healing from this experience? I prevailed in this situation only after we developed another group for her to attend, this time moving beyond abuse to focus on social skills. I wonder how long everyone would have kept her in the group, or maybe she would have just advanced into being one of the leaders as she grew older!

This story hopefully has an obvious point—that as great as healing is, it is a process and not the destination of the journey of life. I have run across many similar stories over the years. I remember the psychologist who was in his own therapy for seven years and was told by his therapist that he was not yet strong enough to stop treatment. There was the professional woman who for years had planned her week not around her business but around her appointments for individual and group therapy several times a week. I have frequently come across people who believe that if some therapy is good, a lot is always better. But I do not believe this to be true.

If healing is a journey and not the desired destination, then what is? For me, the goal is to be free of the chains of the past, not make friends with the chains, polish the chains, or proudly display them as a badge of honor. I believe it is a strategy to make internal peace with anything in our lives that can't be changed or overcome. For many people this can include illness, pain, disability, limitations or genetic traits such as being tall or short. But healing is a process to address an injury and then to move beyond the problem, not to build our lives around the problem, or around the solution to the problem.

Our therapeutically sensitized culture (don't all the rich, the famous, and the beautiful people have therapists?) holds out healing as a success, as it should. But there are no medals we should always wear or trophies that we should carry around throughout life. We can certainly acknowledge both the pain of our past and the courage it took to heal, but now it is time to move on.

Trauma Is Part of the Human Condition

There is no question that, at times, all of our lives present us with situations that are very difficult with which to cope. There are also times that our coping skills are not enough. When we cannot cope and we experience the situation as very physically or psychologically threatening, traumatic experience can be the result. Since there has essentially been no time Homo sapiens have been on the planet that we were ever truly safe, trauma has always been a part of our human condition.

We like to complain that modern living is more stressful and difficult than the "good old days." But just when were the good old days? Perhaps in the roaring 20s when there was an effort to live for the day and enjoy life? But this was right after the first World War, right during the stock market crash where people lost fortunes, their homes, and much of the population of our country was destitute. Perhaps the good old days were the 30s and 40s when the song *Happy Days are Here Again* was popular. But these were years of dramatic changes in the economic fabric of our society due to the effects of the industrial revolution on every aspect of our society. It was also a time of great global unrest that planted the seeds of a second "war to end all wars." Perhaps the good old days were in the 50s. If not why would they call the TV program about this time in America *Happy Days*? While there was a strong attempt in the 50s to believe that everything was getting better and technology would cure most of our problems, what technology brought was the very real concern that nuclear war could end life as we know it on the planet at any time.

A close look will show that there never was a time in the past that mankind was in better shape than we are today. Safety and security are not something we take for granted today, but the further back in time we go, the more tenuous safety appears to be for much of the world's population. It appears that if there ever was a good time to be alive, in respect to healthcare, economic possibilities, human rights, and the rule of law, it is right now. Clearly, some countries provide more of these advantages than others. But even with the growing challenges our present day has—wars, global climate change, overpopulation, genocide and much more—the evidence suggests mankind has collectively never had it so good. These are actually the good old days, if they ever existed.

So if the current age constitute the good old days, why don't they feel so good? The answer seems related to our access to information about the trauma of others. There is the presence all around us of trauma in our lives and the lives of others. On the morning radio news not long ago they announced that a record number of civilians had been killed in Iraq that month, along with the announcement of the 3,000th US soldier killed in the war. A global pandemic is frequently mentioned in the news, as are the effects of global climate change on violent and unusual weather patterns around the globe. As I write this, there was a local death from bird flu, law enforcement agencies were bracing for the fatalities on the highways this holiday season and, oh yes, terrorists are planning major attacks around the world, including in the U.S. The only secure feelings any of us can achieve are when we ignore the reality around us that security is to a large extent an illusion.

We do not feel like these are the good old days in part due to our access to information. There are very bad things that happen around the world, but today we hear and see information about many more of them than we did in the past. Our real time news and information bombards us with what people want to know, and media outlets tell us that people want to know the bad news. As they say in television, "if it bleeds, it leads." So we have more than our own concerns and struggles to cope with; we have the world's traumas coming into our homes all day long— "Welcome to Total News Network coming to you 24-hours-a-day, bad news whenever you need some."

࿇

Out of the tsunami came inspirational stories

During a recent holiday season, an underwater earthquake and tsunami hit the shores of the Indian Ocean and changed the lives of millions and took the lives of 250,000 people. Out of the devastation of such a global catastrophe, there were many rays of hope, not only from the outpouring of aid from around the world but from the traumatized people themselves. One father of eight children sat on the beach in tears saying that his home, his village, his wife and all his children were swept out to sea. But within a week this same man was building a foundation for a home he would share with orphaned children he found wandering amid the destruction. It is clear that some people possess an amazing ability to be resilient. Could it be possible that we all possess this potential?

❧❧

Was there ever such a thing as the good old days? Actually what we have today and always have had is a reality of the human condition that at any time and at any place we are vulnerable to traumatic experiences that could drastically change our lives. Faced with this reality, we must learn how to better cope with what we face, and to learn how to handle traumatic experiences that we cannot avoid.

If You Know Where You Are Going, You Have a Better Chance of Getting There

We are all born with an internal biological compass of where we are going in life, and the instinctive goal is to survive as long as possible. Keeping this in mind helps us throughout life to be on the planet longer. A major aspect of living is to structure our world to eliminate as many threats to our survival as possible. This may seem like a paradox when we consider how many commuters get on freeways each morning and evening of the work week. With the risks we take each day, we do our best to master these risks either physically (we wear seatbelts and have airbags) or psychologically (we tell ourselves the risk is low and that death on the roadways will not be our fate, but tens of thousands are wrong each year). By living this way we are able to do more than be anxious or incapacitated by fear of the many risks involved in living. However, not all risks can be eliminated, and for traumatic events that cannot be prevented we must develop an ability to overcome them, or they will overcome us. Most of us do this with our ability to cope with stress and threats.

If humans have been as successful as they have at surviving in a world of insecurity and threats, we must be doing something right related to facing the struggles in our lives. There is little doubt that humans have been very good at surviving as a species on the planet. In a relatively short time in geological terms, mankind has populated the world, explored and settled the farthest reaches of the globe, and has even been orbiting the planet for many years. Our numbers have increased as a species to the point that our 6 billion members are taxing the resources of our planetary home. But in such a challenging world, how are humans successfully surviving to such a degree the population is nearing a problematic level?

The answer to the above question appears, in part, to be due to the ability of the human brain to adapt to whatever and wherever it finds itself. The prime directive of the brain is to survive. At birth a baby's brain is only 25% developed, leaving the other 75% with the ability to adapt to the challenges the individual will need to overcome. One of the initial vulnerabilities of a human at birth, an oversized head that the body cannot even hold upright for weeks or even months, will eventually be the tool that will make all the difference in surviving. We are all born with one of these very large heads protecting a special brain that is the most complex organic structure in the known universe (one can only hope that one of our space probes may yet find the Vulcans and their more advanced and logical brains). But for now the human brain takes the prize for its ability to problem-solve, develop capacities that go far beyond survival, and even to reflect on itself. The brain is also very good at healing when we understand how to promote this internal strength.

Our Internal Healing Potential

One assessment of the medical advances over the last 20-30 years could be that we have yet to understand the healing potential that we all possess. Particularly in the Western world, we tend to rely more on science, technology and external cures than we do on our own capacity to heal. How often do we hear it said when someone overcomes a life-threatening illness that it was a medical "miracle." In other words, doctors don't know what happened and therefore it must be unexplainable. I have run into situations where a child's neurological improvement has been called a psychiatric miracle. However, just because we don't know how the body did it, does not mean the miracle did not come from within, rather than from without.

In the first chapter we considered how we all have the potential to heal in mind, body and spirit. It can be an empowering experience to trust our own ability to heal. This does not mean that we ignore the oncologist's recommendations for treating our cancer. But it does mean that we will come out ahead if we engage our internal healing power along with external treatments. We will see later that there is amazing power in the way we think about a situation. Regardless of our medical or scientific knowledge, we need to be humble enough to realize that humans have been on the planet for many millennia without Prilosec, Prozac and Viagra. Perhaps we have lived with more heartburn, more down days and with a limp…well, less stamina, but we have nonetheless made it often due to our internal ability to heal and to manage.

Rather than reject science or "better living through chemistry," to me the optimum strategy seems to be to take advantage of the help that is increasingly available to live healthy, productive lives, while seeing external means of promoting health as assistance to our internal ability. I am often asked if I have a position on the use of psychotropic medications, particularly for children. My answer is that I take no philosophical position for or against the concept of medication. The pertinent issue to me is: does it help both in the short and long term? For example, research continues to say that stimulant medication is the most efficacious treatment of diagnosable hyperactivity in adults, teens and children, even very young children below school age. Unlike anti-medication groups, and a few movie stars, I am very interested in what actually works. However, I think we are missing the point if we rely on a pill to get the job done without utilizing our internal ability to aid in the solution. What this can mean, using the example of hyperactivity, is to give a child the stimulant medication in addition to developing the child's skills at self-regulation and telling the child, "this pill will help you do all the things you need to do to be in charge of your body." Such an approach, it seems to me, helps in the short and long term.

∾

Lenny wanted to do it on his own

Lenny listened when we talked about his Ritalin not being the answer but an aid to develop more internal control. After five months of treatment Lenny asked to talk to me and he said, "I think I can show self-control without my meds, and I would like a chance to prove it." I was impressed with his sincerity. His psychiatrist thought he was not quite ready, but he was

*soon given the chance to demonstrate the ability to
manage his body without the familiar little white pill he
had taken for years. When he got the chance, he did
show us that his internal desire was as strong as the
medication. Since my experience with Lenny, I always
listen for the child who thinks he or she can self-manage
without medication. Sometimes they are correct and
this type of self-confidence is always a plus.*

ॐॐ

The Body's Own Pharmacy

Speaking of medications and how they can help in
healing, we are beginning to notice that our bodies have
had the ability to medicate from within all along. As the
master control center of the body, the human brain controls
a built-in pharmacy that can facilitate homeostasis
(maintaining equilibrium), as well as allostasis (enabling
arousal and returning to baseline). The body's pharmacy
involves chemical alterations in cells as well as alteration of
entire body systems. When the body is functioning well, the
chemical structures influenced by the brain are designed to
keep a complex organism working smoothly. The body's
drug store is the prototype for the pharmacy we visit in our
local neighborhood. It is only when the body's pharmacy is
misfiring in some way that we need to supplement our
naturally produced drugs from an external source.

The types of drugs naturally produced by a healthy
body will sound familiar. There are steroids, opioids,
antidepressants, stimulants, analgesics, anesthesics,
antihistamines, and hundreds of others. If you watch
primetime television and see all the ads asking you to, "ask
your doctor about our prescription medication," the odds
are that the body can internally produce something very

similar. But drug companies do not make money on promoting activation of internal medications.

పోల

Attachment promotes pain relief

Social support and attachment, in particular, appear to assist the body to metabolize negative emotions and help the person frame the traumatic event into their core belief system or inner working model. Of course the opposite is also true that the lack of attachment increases the stress of traumatic situations by blocking the body's ability to handle negative emotions. The body is prepared to go a step further, and, during the dissociative response to stress, the brain releases endogenous opioids to relieve pain (Neborsky, 2003). In the same way that negative factors can come together to compound a problem, social support, a positive outlook, and self-mastery skills can all come together to make a profound difference in our experience and success in life.

పోల

Without providing a lesson in biochemistry or endocrinology, the body's pharmacy impacts every region and system of the body from the neurological system, to the digestive, respiratory, reproductive and even the skeletal systems. The neurological system relies on the chemical transfer of neuron activity through 52 known neurotransmitters. Many of these are familiar, such as dopamine and serotonin. Others, such as tyrosine, L-dopa, and epinephrine, are much less known. However, all have specific functions that influence the activity of the cells and bodily systems. Neurotransmitters such as endorphins are the body's analgesics or pain relievers; dopamine helps produce emotional experiences such as pleasure. The modern psychotrophic medications are modeled after what the body has the ability to produce on its own.

Hormones are another aspect of the body's pharmacy. These include the steroids, amino acids and eicosanoids (Marieb, 1995). Hormones are produced in glands throughout the body such as the pituitary, adrenal, thyroid, pancreas and others. Hormones have many functions in the body, but all are designed to aid in healthy functioning.

I have included this short treatment of the body's pharmacy because many people are surprised to learn that the body produces a wide range of drugs such as opiods that are similar in chemical composition and function to botanical and laboratory-produced opium. The main point is that the body has an amazing ability to heal itself, to medicate itself, and to find equilibrium to promote survival. When our internal drug store senses medications coming from the outside, it can shut down production, sometimes forever. Our culture, in my opinion, has come to rely too much on external drugs and not enough on the body's ability to heal itself.

Healing Is a Process, Not a Destination

Healing is a necessary way to get to the desired destination, a vehicle to take us where we want to go. Many individuals who have experienced trauma have their dreams and hopes in life shattered. Certainly if we stay in a traumatized place, we can forget about reaching our true potential. This is where healing is critically important. However, too many people who have gone through significant trauma, and too many people who help them in the process, forget that healing is not their full potential but rather a necessary process to regain hope in reaching full potential and a positive future.

The tendency of human beings is to define ourselves and others by what we have been through, by how we are different than others, or by some disability. We consider some people alcoholics, rather than people with alcoholism. We talk about a disabled person rather than a person challenged by a disability. This may seem a subtle difference in terminology, but it is a major difference in meaning. Is the blind woman defined by the fact that she does not have sight as others do? Is an epileptic the same as someone who has epilepsy? The major difference in thinking is in definition. We do not all have obvious disabilities, but at times in our lives all of us have others define us by some event, some condition, or some challenge that does not come close to defining who we are as individuals. It is even more troubling when the individual self-defines by some characteristic or condition.

I have worked over the years with people in the process of dying. This can be very instructive to see how people handle being around someone facing imminent death, and to see how the person facing death handles this as well. I have always felt that dying is one time in your life that you should be able to do it your way. However, I am always struck by the person who gives into the temptation to be defined by the dying process. Equally poignant is the dance where the family or medical staff do not tell the person that they are about to die. This is just another way to have the significance of the dying process take over our experience for us, rather than us determining our experience. Of all the conditions that people find themselves facing, dying is hard to ignore and equally hard to get beyond its symbolic stature. We all have to die, but some people are busy being the dying person days, months or even years before the time comes. There are others who know that death may be at the door but are too busy living to answer the door just yet; death may just have to wait until they have lived a bit longer.

I used the parallel with the dying process and healing process because although both are required of us, we have some say over whether it defines us or we define it. Healing is a great rest stop along the highway of life, but don't get so used to the rest stop that you forget to get back on the highway toward your dreams and your potential.

Breaking Through the Limitations of Trauma

If we are going to really live, we need to not be too distracted with the inevitability that we will die at some point. At the same time, there is a Far Eastern saying that to fully appreciate living, keep death just over your shoulder. Or as the Zen master commented to the student, "See this glass, when I look at it I see it already broken so I appreciate it all the more while it is whole." This points out the balance of living; we can neither be overwhelmed with the inevitability of death to the point we cease to fully live, nor can we live in denial that life will keep getting better all the time, and there will always be another day, another month or another year — because at some point there will not be.

To reach our potential, we must move beyond the symbolic importance of events in our lives. We never forget our favorite pet that died when we were growing up, but such a significant event cannot mute our ability to live fully, including the possibility of embracing another pet at some point. There is always a temptation to be overwhelmed, stuck, or defined by things that we face in life. Trauma is one of the most tempting life events that can do this.

It may be a fact that so few people fully heal from trauma that we as a society have held up limited goals and expectations for people who have faced traumatic experiences. Perhaps we can get over losing a pet as a child, but can we go through the trauma of losing a child? Such an experience is often said to be the hardest thing anyone can face in life. Some who have faced this have said that they emerged more dead than alive afterward. While we can understand this, we certainly hate to see this happen. I have used death in several examples, but there are many little deaths involved in living. It is our attachment to loved ones that makes it so difficult to let go when we have no choice. But we get attached to more than loved ones and pets, we get attached to our routines, our familiar patterns of living, and our internal sense of safety and security. Traumatic experiences can quickly rob us of such attachments. When trauma takes away our familiar patterns of loving, we grieve not entirely differently than when a loved one dies. We wonder if we can go on, and if it makes any sense to go on.

Trauma brings with it an experience of a type of death. We have lost something special; at the least we are not able to go back to how life was before the trauma. Trauma can bring with it major changes in our lives. It can make us feel as if we are no longer ourselves. It can make us think, feel and act differently so that we don't know who we are any longer. Trauma can change our sense of meaning and purpose in life, usually in a negative direction. In a sense, these are some of the emotional, psychological and even spiritual impacts of trauma. Trauma can change (seldom in a positive way) how our brains respond to the world around us. Trauma can impact us in ways we don't even realize or notice. There is no question that traumatic experiences can bring many potential limitations to the person involved. It must be the goal of traumatized individuals to overcome or reduce the impact of the limitations to fully live the rest of their lives.

As helpers we have a careful balance to strike in our support of those who have experienced trauma. We cannot act like motivational speakers in an auditorium of business people. That would not be supportive. But neither can we permanently wrinkle our brows and say how incredibly sorry we are that the individual is going through what he or she is facing. This approach can support the person in being unable to move much beyond the task of taking in another breath or getting through another day.

We must have the true supportive empathy exhibited by a mother I once worked with. She had a young child who was blinded in an accident. In my office the boy dropped a toy; I immediately wanted to pick it up for the him. This would have made me feel better and eliminated my stress in the situation. However, the mother motioned me away. There was a pause while the boy waited for someone to step in and hand him the toy. When no one did, he asked for help. His mother said, "I know you can find it on your own." She loved her child enough to teach him how to fish rather than hand him a fish, and in doing so she taught him to be a little more independent. I found her strength a real inspiration in the face of the symbolic heaviness of a child dealing with having no sight. I ask myself often if I am strong enough to help others work with their own forms of blindness.

It must be the goal of all of us who help traumatized individuals to set the bar high in overcoming the limitations of a traumatic event. Some people are self-starters and you can't keep them down if you try. But most people, this is particularly true of children, pick up from others a sense of how far they can be expected to go, and how high they will be able to fly. As helpers we must encourage these individuals to set their goals high.

THE PATH TO HEALING

Healing is a process but not a destination.

Coping with bad events is an essential skill.

The brain is the key to surviving and thriving.

Learn to harness the power of internal healing.

Combine external and internal healing aids.

Expand ways to produce internal medications.

Don't let any experience or limitation define who you are.

Keep the bar high when it comes to internal expectations.

THREE

THE SURVIVOR TRAP

It may seem unlikely that surviving a potentially life-threatening or significant traumatic event could end up negatively restricting one's future, but this is possible with trauma. Because traumatic experiences can have a profound impact on both the individual's present and future, it is important to move from being a victim of the situation to being a survivor. However, to align oneself solely as a survivor can come to define the person and inadvertently bring its own limitations. The only part of a traumatic experience to incorporate into one's self-definition is that the person overcame the obstacles and came out ahead. Anything less than this can become a trap, or what I call the survivor trap.

The survivor trap occurs when someone carries through life the traumatic event in such a way as to distract from personal goals or add additional burdens to daily living. Just the act of frequently thinking about significant negative events in our lives can have an adverse impact on our attitude and energy. This is not to suggest that taking the time to celebrate the fact that we have survived and overcome the challenge of the experience is a bad thing. But as any artist, athlete or scientist has found, resting on the laurels of past accomplishments is not the foundation for future success. There is the East Indian expression that says "when you get a thorn stuck in your foot, you take another thorn to get it out, but then you throw both thorns away." To avoid the survivor trap, it is important to limit the impact of the trauma on our lives and our future.

What Is Wrong with Being a Survivor?

There is no argument that being a survivor is far better than being a victim. So what is wrong with being a survivor? There are many ways this question could be answered, but it all comes down to one word: power, or more precisely, the lack of power. It is power that produces the long-term negative impact of a traumatic experience. If two people find themselves in the same situation and one has the ability to impact the situation and the other person is powerless to do anything, the person who is likely to end up traumatized is predictable—the powerless individual.

Power is at the base of traumatic experience in the first place. Trauma is any situation that overwhelms our ability to cope with the situation. The inability to cope comes from the absence of the ability to respond, to change, to influence, to understand, or to get out of a frightening or intensely negative experience. Therefore the inability to cope relates to powerlessness.

Power appears to be one explanation for why some soldiers are traumatized by war and others are not. Power relates to more than just the physical ability to respond to a situation. Internal power is also very important when it comes to trauma because trauma is also predicated on the way the individual perceives the situation. So the power over our internal experience—our emotions, our perceptions and our conceptual understanding—can all greatly influence whether we have a traumatic experience. So power and powerlessness are at the root of both the initial experience of trauma and the short and long-term impact of the experience.

From a power perspective, what is wrong with being a survivor? To move from feeling like a victim to a survivor takes courage, support and personal power. At the same time, to move from being defined as a survivor to being free of the past takes even more power. To reach our full potential as individuals we need to take advantage of our experiences and our past, but we also need to be careful as to which experiences we allow to define us or, for that matter, to limit us. It is very tempting to have a traumatic experience define us in some way. There are two ways an experience can have power over us, either in a negative way or positive way. Certainly being defined in a positive way is preferable to negative, but the experience still has power over the individual rather than the individual having power over the experience.

To have power over any experience in life involves the decision of moving on and relegating the experience to the past. This does not mean to block an experience from our memory either in a conscious or subconscious way. As many traumatized individuals have found, blocking memories actually gives the memories power over the individual because it is never clear when a blocked memory will be triggered from subconscious to conscious awareness. When we act as if it does not exist, this does not make it go away; it just means we are pretending to have power over the memory, but this is not true power.

True power over an experience is to relegate the experience to the importance we want it to have. It takes true internal power to define our pasts and our selves as we choose, rather than have our pasts define us. If someone who has experienced some form of trauma chooses to build his or her self-definition around the experience, I support this entirely. For example, there are times that major events just happen to take place before us. Examples could be witnessing the assassination of President Kennedy in Dallas, or being present on Iwo Jima as the marines raised the flag, or personally witnessing the collapse of the World Trade Center, as thousands did on September 11, 2001. Whether positive or negative, some people chose to include such major events as a part of their personal life resume. When this is a conscious choice, the person is using their power of self-definition.

❧❦

Judith did not fight her past, she fought city hall — and won!

As a child Judith was abused and neglected for many of her early years. Because her own family let her down, she headed into the world of foster care. She was placed in home after home, not because she was difficult, but because she could not find a place where she was loved and where she belonged. Many of her needs were met in foster care, but not all. She had much within her that needed to heal and she pursued this healing as an adult with the same tenacity she showed in home after home growing up. I ran into Judith when we worked together in her healing process. Her spirit was impressive and contagious to others who faced the steep road of healing from abuse. As she moved from victim to survivor, she wanted more. In considering her life she went back looking for information to fill the empty gaps of years of wandering in the foster care system. She found only her tracks and no information because it was all destroyed. No pictures, report cards, or records of any sort. She had a childhood that had been shredded like someone's old bank statements. Judith felt empty for a short time and then focused her energy to work on this unfair situation. In the process she would change her own life and the lives of others like her. Through her persistence, she was able to convince one decision-maker, then two, and finally the entire State Legislature to change the laws so no other child's history was shredded and forgotten. Judith looked for her past and ended up changing the future for children she will never meet.

❧❦

Defining oneself as a survivor of trauma is not always a choice. Some view this as the more positive of only two choices — victim or survivor. However, I propose that we help those who have experienced trauma broaden their choices. To fully use internal power, the choices need to include not only victim or survivor but also the choice to acknowledge, grieve as necessary, and relegate the experience to the past and choose not to have the experience define the individual in any way. As long as traumatized individuals have this third choice, whether they choose it or not, I support their ability to decide how they decide to view the experience.

Based on the previous points, being a survivor may be a very positive and healthy choice, or it may not be. The difference is whether the individual has actually made a decision and considered the alternatives available. Being a survivor is only a trap if we are stuck in a self-defining situation that we did not choose, or even more so, that we are unaware of.

A Personal Trauma

Everyone is vulnerable to traumatic experiences. The risks involved in our world are very real, but we consider many of these risks to be routine and give them little consideration. In this way, we attempt to ignore the risks hoping to make them somehow less real. Most of us do this every time we drive a car. We have no idea if the next person coming at us just left the bar, is impaired by a new prescription, or is falling asleep at the wheel in our lane of traffic. We don't like to think that all drivers by the nature of being on the road, enter the highway lottery where over 50,000 will die each year. If the odds of surviving a plane flight were anywhere near the odds of surviving a drive to the mall, we would have shorter lines in airports. But, in the hope of making the risk less real, we don't think of everyday risks such as driving. However, regardless of what we tell ourselves, bad things happen to everyone.

Let me share a personal experience here. I actually feel blessed that I have had a minimum of traumatic experiences in my life. The few I have had do not compare with those of the many traumatized men, women and children I have been fortunate to work with over the years. Although this experience was not a life-threatening event or any type of abuse, it fits the definition of a trauma. Some would call it traumatic grief. But my relating this story will give me a chance to make several points about healing. As I wrote this last sentence I had to stop and consider whether I really did want to share this experience. It is not the self-disclosure that caused me pause, because I believe it may help make the points I want to get across. No, the pause was about whether I wanted to reopen a deep and personal wound, not unlike the wounds of the past that we all have. After taking a break, I have decided to proceed and share the experience.

I received a call nearly 30 years ago regarding an individual with whom I had one of the closest relationships at that point in my life or will ever have. My friend was hit by a car while riding a bike. The good news was that my dear friend would survive the experience; the bad news was that he was terribly injured and would need multiple surgeries to repair his broken body as well as his head trauma and anticipated brain injury. He lived in a state far away so I was not able to be involved in his healing (part of my sense of powerlessness). Over the following months as he learned all over again to walk, to speak, and attempted to understand what had happened (he had no memory of the accident), it was clear that he lost most of his memory of me, our relationship, and even who he used to be. So my experience was that his body had survived being hit by the car and the extensive period of recovery, but had the person I knew survived? When we talked on the phone, he sounded different, he spoke differently, and it was not clear to me whether he was just being polite in saying that he remembered who I was. My inability to reach out and help him regain our mutual relationship contributed to my growing sense of being powerless to help him.

Consistent with many individuals with significant head trauma, his personality had changed as well as his sense of himself and the world. Before the accident, he was a loving and highly charismatic individual with the ability to look deeply into the eyes of someone, and the experience led some people to feel as if he was touching their soul. He was a healer by profession and one of the best who ever walked this planet. But after the accident he was withdrawn, moody and prone to dark periods of depression and self-loathing. He had the best of psychiatric care, but the treating psychiatrist told me there was only so much anyone could do after such a personality- and life-changing tragedy.

As someone who professionally helped traumatized individuals, I felt intense personal pressure to be of help in some way. I worked to arrange for him to visit our family and live with us for awhile. The psychiatrist balked at the prospect because my friend had grown increasingly unstable and had talked of suicide. I was even more persistent to have him come and heal with me rather than be in and out of the psychiatric hospital. Perhaps it was some desperation on the part of the psychiatrist, but I thought I was beginning to convince him that living with me would potentially do some good. It was right at that point that I received the call from his family that he was gone. He had gone into a gun store, purchased a handgun, and with no hesitation, left the store and shot himself in the head.

With tears in my eyes as I write this, I remember it was as if someone hit the pause button on my world during that phone call. Time stood still; there was nothing I could do to change what had happened, and there was nothing left that held any real importance. I remember the tears; I remember the emptiness, the guilt, and the anger. I also remember the loss of a sense of time that lasted well over a six-month period as I attempted to live my life, because everything was now different.

My healing took years and involved personal and professional support. My journey had to include connection with his family, allowing my inner grief to be expressed, gaining spiritual support so I could forgive my inability to be of help, and perhaps most importantly, I had to develop an understanding of the events that had occurred to him and to me. I had to gain at least the power to understand in order to go on with my life.

Reading between the lines you can tell that this was not just a friend; in fact, I have never even used the term friend to describe him. He was a spiritual healer, he was a teacher and mentor to me, and he was able to look into my soul and teach me to find my internal source of divine love and find this source in others. At other times and in other cultures, this man would have been called a seer, a guru, a prophet. But he was always unassuming, terribly out of fashion in the way he dressed and acted, and was humble to a fault. How could such a person end his own life with a gun, and bring so much grief to all who knew him? Over time my healing led me to understand that the man I knew could not have done this. The man I knew was killed when he was hit by the car. The individual who had survived was someone else, the result of desperate medical efforts to patch together his body and brain. The individual who took his life did not really remember me, his previous life, or why he was living in someone else's body.

I did not plan to write all this, but I have allowed myself to do so. It has not only been another step in my own healing from this trauma, but it seems that it can be of some help to consider the healing process and beyond. I just looked up the date, and the above events happened 26 years, 7 months and

6 days in the past. However, events like these have no real position in time. It could have been yesterday as far as my experience, my memories, and my spirit are concerned.

The above experience will always be a part of me. I do not share this to say it was either more or less traumatic than events you have been through. Trauma defies measurement or comparison. For me, this experience was more than I could cope with at the time. I was powerless to change these events. Although I was professionally someone who helped others with trauma, even, at times, head trauma, I was impotent in this case to help someone I loved more deeply in a way than I loved myself. My job was to heal myself and then go forward with my life.

There are several hints at how I went about healing this trauma. I had to involve my mind, my body and my spirit in the healing process. This was not a conscious choice, it was necessary. I had to heal myself of my guilt in being powerless to help. I had to heal my mind in understanding why and how all this could have happened the way it did. I had to let the emotional and physical pain express itself alone and with others I relied on for support at the time.

The fact that it still brings tears today, and can be very real and painful still, does not indicate to me that my healing has been insufficient. To the contrary, the fact that I can allow such a profoundly impactful experience into my mental and emotional awareness and express what comes up in words, sensations, and tears is a sign of true healing. I have not consciously moved beyond healing from this traumatic time in my life; it came naturally and gradually. But I have not stopped with healing, I have moved on.

These events do not take energy from me each day. In fact, although they are available at any time, they may not be called to mind for months or longer at a time. I have chosen not to ritualize this experience in any way; I don't remember the date of his death because to me his death was many months earlier due to the accident. I do think about the person I knew several times a week but more to remember what he taught me, and his final chapter does not enter into this process. And here is the point of this extended description of a personal trauma in my life: when trauma happens, let yourself express what is real, be patient and caring to yourself, ask for support from others, seek professional help if you wish, put the experience in words, thoughts and feelings, heal as long as necessary — then move on.

But what does "move on" mean? The answer to this important question will be reflected in various ways throughout this book. Briefly stated, moving on from trauma is to ensure that the traumatic experience adds a challenging component to your life, but it must not hinder you from attaining your potential. Nothing you want to do with your life would add to your life satisfaction that should be prevented in any way by trauma you have experienced. I realize that some trauma, such as war or serious physical abuse, can cause long-term physical difficulties or disabilities. But even when life throws us a difficult challenge such as a serious illness or physical disability, we have the potential to incorporate this new reality into our revised hopes and dreams.

Moving on from a traumatic experience could include incorporating the experience into your future in a specific way. For example, Lance Armstrong responded to his life-threatening trauma of testicular cancer in a way that has inspired people around the world. He fought the disease and came back from it to physically perform even better than he had before, due to his motivation and internal inspiration. And he incorporated cancer into his world in a positive way to model healing and triumph over physical disease. In this way he has become one of the world's most well-known symbols of cancer recovery and personification of succeeding in life despite the greatest of hardships. Lance Armstrong was transformed by his traumatic fight with cancer in nearly every way. His body changed, his will-power changed, his personality may even have changed in some ways. Perhaps the least of his accomplishments are the ones he is best known for—winning bicycle races, as impressive as these were. His greatest accomplishment was to overcome the limitations that his physical disease could have placed on his future, his dreams, and his outlook on life.

Being a Survivor Is Part of Your Resume, Not a Statement of Your Limits

Lance Armstrong is an excellent example of not only surviving a life threatening trauma, but incorporating this experience into a new chapter in his life that has given him the potential to literally inspire millions of people and thus change the world. No amount of skill in riding a bicycle could have given him the power to influence so many. But he is not alone in refusing to allow a traumatic experience to limit his life. Only after his death did most of us learn that wounds received in a traumatic experience in the military should have prevented a young John Fitzgerald Kennedy from the grueling physical demands of campaigning for public office, or the demands of being leader of the free world. Yet he endured, and he also changed the world. Agnes Gonxha Bojaxhiu, otherwise known as Mother Teresa, was not the victim of a specific traumatic experience, but she faced the limitations of her frail physical stature and ill health most of her life. Several times she was ordered under her vow of obedience to take care of herself and leave feeding the hungry, clothing the naked, and comforting the dying of the world to others with more strength and health. However, she overcame her limitations and also changed the world, helping one person at a time. Long after her death she will continue to inspire and play a direct role in improving the lives of millions of poor throughout the world.

All three are examples of people who refused to allow challenges, such as trauma in life, to place any limits on their potential. At the same time, all three would fiercely disagree that what they did was in any way heroic. First, all three would say they did what they could when faced with what they were dealt in life. All three would credit the support from others who sustained them during their personal battles. All three would deny that they did anything special other than to live each day as they felt they must. The ability to move on from the limitations of difficult or traumatic experiences may be one of the few similarities of these three very different people—a frail nun born in Macedonia, a skinny rich kid from Massachusetts, and a bicycle rider from Texas. If these three settled for less in life, had accepted the obvious limitations their situations placed on their dreams, then all of us would be poorer for it.

Few of us have the ability or desire to change the world. That should not be the goal. But we can have the goal of fully living our lives in a way that seeks to fulfill our potential. To do this we cannot permanently pull over to the rest stop of being simply a "trauma survivor."

The Brain After a Traumatic Experience

To avoid negative influences of traumatic experience we need to have some understanding of how the brain is affected by trauma. Since the brain is genetically and instinctively set to promote the survival of the individual, anything that threatens survival will be a priority to the brain. It is not necessary that an experience actually be life-threatening, it merely needs to be perceived as life-threatening. This distinction is critical because many young children start life out with the powerless experience of running into threats for which they have no defense. It also appears that the brain is more seriously impacted the younger the individual is. The combination of a young helpless child facing a perceived threat to survival, along with the adaptation of the brain starting off so early in life, can come together to provide "the perfect storm" of adverse neuro-psychological development of the brain.

The adaptation responses of the brain to the environment sets in motion physical changes in the brain's structure as well as chemical changes in how the brain takes in and processes new information. A couple of examples may be helpful to show this.

I will begin with changes in the brain's structure related to non-threatening experiences early in life. Since the brain of a child is only 25% developed at birth, it uses the other 75% depending on what is needed to adapt and achieve survival. As a child comes into the world and begins a series of instinctual signals to the environment such as: I am cold; I am hungry; I am tired; I am in pain; the brain of the child is working three times as efficiently as an adult brain in perceiving the response coming back. The brain knows there is no time to lose, one unmet need (a blocked airway for example) might mean death. So when the brain picks up signals that the environment takes care of the cold, the hunger, and other needs, the brain responds by setting off a sequence of proximity-seeking positive behaviors designed to elicit instinctive care-taking behavior and emotions from the mother (the environment). What is going on in the brain is that synaptic connections are being developed very rapidly and are being strengthened each time a need is successfully met. In this way the trillions of "hard wired" connections in the brain are literally affecting the physical structure of the brain.

Staying with a positive scenario, the adaptive ability of the brain to structure itself around the environment now moves to the chemical processes that take advantage of the physical structures that are rapidly developing in the brain. When basic needs are met, the brain releases calming neuro-transmitters such as dopamine that help shut down stress hormones signaled by basic needs coming to the attention of the brain.

If you observe an infant, there is little subtlety in behavior related to needs. When a basic need arises, the child lets the caretakers know this by full scale, maximum volume crying or screaming. The brain is not yet sophisticated enough to know when the system is just a little thirsty, very thirsty or near-death thirsty, so when the need comes into awareness, the safe course is to go all out to have the need met. When the need is met, the brain activity signals the release of neurotransmitters that turn off the emotional/behavior signals and the child moves on to the next need the brain senses. When the needs are successfully met, the brain remembers the source of the comfort (the care provider), and the brain quickly makes sure it remembers just which one of these adults is the one that best meets basic needs when they come up. If all this sounds a bit mechanistic and impersonal, it actually is in the early stages of life. However, this imprinting, instinctual dance of the child and parent can move quickly into a positive symbiotic attachment with needs being met on both sides. In the other scenario, needs are not met and a very different result can come from the adaptive response of the brain (Ziegler, 2006).

I will not repeat the entire process described above when the brain determines that the environment is not responding adequately to meet the survival needs of the child. However, in the same way that positive adaptations come from needs being met, very different adaptations result when needs are not adequately provided. The brain knows the situation: without external help the child will quickly die. Again, there is no time to be patient and see if things improve over time if a need is not immediately met. The child's system goes into crisis mode with even small needs, the emotional/behavioral signals are sent out to the environment in the form of intense crying or screaming and the brain picks up what comes back. If the environment responds with pain, yelling, the wrong solution, or perhaps —the worst response of all—indifference, the brain goes into a new level of crisis mode. It now believes that survival is imminently threatened. It begins to push away from anyone providing inadequate care and the stress response related to every perceived need becomes heightened. When this pattern begins to happen, the child experiences stress constantly, the brain releases stress hormones and the child gives the world another chance to help by constant indications of unhappiness.

But some traumatic experiences happen much later in life, even in adulthood. I have used the example of an infant to show how the brain adapts both structurally and chemically. But to a lesser degree, the brains of older children and even adults also adapt to traumatic experiences later in life. How an individual's brain responds to trauma later in life has a lot to do with how the individual's needs were met early in life. The brain develops a positive expectation from the environment based on needs being repeatedly met. We might call this the beginning of an optimistic view of life. However, the brain develops a pessimistic orientation toward the environment if early experiences were of needs not being met. It is very frequent that early pessimistic experiences can plague the child, teen and adult for years due to an early-developed negative inner working model of unmet needs. This appears to be the reason why early childhood neglect has the most serious long-term impact of any time of trauma.

In older children or even adults, the brain responds to traumatic experience by adapting and making structural and chemical changes. The limbic system comes into play as the emotion/fear/trauma memory center of the brain. A traumatized adult will likely face the challenge of the amydala making its presence known frequently after the trauma. For example, after someone experiences serious mechanical problems in a plane causing a frightening emergency landing, the amygdala will be very sensitized on future flights to turbulence, the landing gear coming down, or perhaps even buying the ticket and thinking about being in such a vulnerable position again. The limbic system will involuntarily remember such an event and, because the brain perceived the threat to survival (which was very real at 30,000 feet), anything that reminds the limbic system of such an event will produce hyper-arousal of the stress response.

The brain's ability to modulate the amygdala and limbic system must come from the pre-frontal cortex. Here is the source of self-regulation, modifying emotions, maintaining social support, and finding meaning in life's difficulties. It may be the answer to why some individuals develop Posttraumatic Stress Disorder and others do not. Those individuals who develop long-term problems from trauma may be the ones who have not learned to use the prefrontal cortex to integrate social, emotional, bodily and autobiographical aspects of life (Soloman & Siegal, 2003).

For a more complete discussion of the brain and trauma, I refer you to *Traumatic Experience And The Brain* (Ziegler, 2002).

ॐॐ

Sometimes it helps to have been there.

I started my counseling career as something of a young prodigy. Some young people play a musical instrument beyond what is expected, others grasp math or languages in a way that pleases and surprises their teachers. Although I gave it a shot, music was not my gift and languages other than English were outright failures for me rather than successful ventures. For me, it was quickly grasping the skills and intuition to understand others and relate to them in a way that helped. I was a natural at counseling. I progressed quickly, learned many therapy styles and systems, and I was blessed with excellent teachers, some of the best anywhere. One of these supervisors saw the raw talent I had but was very hard on me as a supervisor. He told me once that I was obviously good, but I would never be an exceptional therapist. When I asked him why, he said, "Because you have never known despair." I found that an odd concept and attributed it to the supervisor's advancing years and a reflection of his struggle and depression about aging and goals he had given up reaching. Several years later after the personal trauma I describe earlier in this chapter, I understood the wisdom of what this supervisor was saying. How could I visit the world of another human being's despair if I had never been there myself? I made an internal pledge that I would listen more intently and take more seriously the despair of others because now I knew something of desolation and at least a taste of despair. I told myself I must use this personal trauma for the good of others and, therefore, myself. I have done my best to stay true to this pledge.

How Do We Move on From a Trauma that Has Changed Our Lives?

This is too complex a question to give a simplistic answer. Everything in this book addresses this question. There are some general statements that can be made about not getting caught in trauma to the point that our lives are diminished. Although much of what we will be considering in these pages is the importance of going beyond healing, healing must come first. In fact, stabilization must come before healing. When a frightening experience overwhelms our ability to cope with the situation, first we must get ourselves in a safe and predictable environment where our brain will stop perceiving threats and signaling the body to be in alarm mode. It is often helpful to surround ourselves with our support system, because support is one of the major ways an individual calms down the internal stress responses. These steps could be considered the stabilization phase.

Next we head into the healing phase, which has already been discussed in some detail. It is important not to rush this step of recovering from a traumatic experience, but it is equally important not to make the healing phase your new home. From here we can launch the steps to move on with our lives.

Since a person is made up of mind, body, and spirit, all three aspects of the person can be utilized in moving forward from trauma. Because of the pivotal role played by the brain during and after trauma, the mind is perhaps the most critical part of the person to address. Healing from trauma depends on how the mind perceives the trauma. We can enlist this same mental dynamic to continually remind ourselves that the trauma is in our past. This is very difficult for children, and is why they need an adult to help their brain realize that the trauma is not still happening in the present.

Our bodies can help by focusing on two very important processes. The first is to engage in activities that bring enjoyment. One of the very serious results of traumatic experiences is to take away the individual's enjoyment of life; this is especially true for young children. We must go out of our way to have fun, pursue pleasurable activities, and involve others to enhance our enjoyment. Forcing ourselves to go out and have fun is about like trying to get physically active when we are depressed. This is the last thing the depressed want to do, but it may be one of the best things they could be doing to lighten their load considerably. Just like depressed people, traumatized people must invest extra energy to engage in life, get active, have fun and do with others what they enjoy.

The spirit comes into play because, at a core level, our spiritual beliefs are what sustain us in life. Whether it is prayer, awareness, being present or other spiritual practices, our spirit can help us to move forward in life after a very challenging experience. Meditation in all its many forms has been found to enhance our awareness, increase our appreciation, improve our mental clarity, and even heighten our productivity. After trauma we may need to spend some time with the global questions such as, "Why me?" Every individual is different, but some level of alignment of the spirit is important to be able to move on from trauma.

Moving on does not mean that we must forget what has happened. In all likelihood we will never forget, nor should we. But we must work to put the experience into its proper or preferred context in the overall picture of our life. It was a very difficult time, or perhaps the worst period of our life, but it was only a part of our past, and it need not be a prominent part of our present and future. There is more to say about moving on from a traumatic experience in the pages ahead.

Why We Lower Our Expectations of Trauma-Damaged People

We all want to support our friends, family, and our clients who have faced trauma and are trying to put their lives back together after the experience. To do so we must confront the fact that we often lower our expectations of someone after such an experience. "John has never been the same since the Vietnam war, poor guy." "Heather won't go out after dark anymore since she was raped." "Charles avoids water sports since the boating accident." Such responses to a traumatic experience are understandable, or even predictable. We want to be understanding and empathetic of the person's feelings, and the last thing we want to do is put pressure on someone or be perceived as being insensitive. So we stand back while trauma survivors seriously alter their lives and avoid perceived threats that may once have been very positive aspects of their lives — water recreation, nightlife, even relationships with others.

In a real sense we lower our expectations of traumatized individuals because of our empathy. If we could put ourselves in their place, we would avoid planes, boats, or be afraid of the dark as well. But is our empathy in such situations helping the other person? There is no universal answer to this question, but I am suggesting that we consider that a traumatized brain will take a predictable and self-protective course of action — avoid people, places or situations that could cause a trauma to be repeated. When this becomes severe we call it a mental health disorder, Posttraumatic Stress Disorder. Something becomes a disorder when it prevents someone from living life in a functional or desirable way. The route to psychological treatment of a brain that is avoiding reminders of trauma is to help the individual reclaim the ability to choose what is wanted in life without losing free choice due to past bad experiences.

I think we can be empathetic and sensitive to others (and ourselves) and not lower our expectations of their ability to live the life they wanted before their trauma. If everyone around the avoidant person simply agrees with them that avoiding the water, or the dark, or ever becoming sexually intimate again makes sense, the individual will likely live and die with traumatic stress. To support and help someone else recover and move on from trauma, I think we need to look at our empathetic response to the person. I think we need to be willing to risk that the individual will be upset with us or even avoid us. But how loving is it to allow someone to stay in their self-created prison, which is what PTSD can become? The balanced approach might be to support the individual, not the fears—to want the best for the person and point out how their reactivity to trauma has robbed him or her of opportunities and potential happiness in his or her life. As in psychological treatment, the brain must be shown a better way, and if we are successful at this, the brain will generally move toward what it perceives as best for the individual. But the important point is that the supportive help of a friend or the skilled work of a trauma therapist can help the individual begin to operate from the high reasoning centers of the brain and not operate from the reactive fear center of the brain.

I hope it has been obvious that when I have mentioned helping someone, that someone may be you helping yourself. It is the same process in confronting the avoidance, the loss of drive toward your potential. Sometimes the friend you must help is yourself.

Trauma Can Bring Physical Scars

Most of the examples I have used have discussed the lingering psychological issues of a traumatic experience. But the aftermath of trauma can be much more than psychological. As I was writing this section I went to a jewelry boutique to pick up a birthday gift for my wife and partner of 40 years. I looked around and chose a necklace and earring set of light green peridot. The woman who came to help me said that she liked my choice and that the jewelry was her design and her handiwork. As I paid for the set, she announced somewhat proudly that she was a brain cancer survivor. I could not help but take that opportunity to briefly discuss with her the premise of this book, that to move beyond being a survivor can open up new paths to personal contentment.

She explained to me that she had two serious surgeries within the last year and the results were both good and bad. The bad aspects were the lingering brain damage that had affected her speech, her hearing on one side and several functions of the left hemisphere of her brain. I reminded her that she was going to share the good part of the surgery. She said that when the left hemisphere of her brain was damaged the right hemisphere was enhanced, and she had noticed an increase in her creativity. She said my wife would be a beneficiary of her brain trauma with the design I had chosen! As I thanked her for her workmanship and for sharing some of her story, I walked away impressed by her method of moving beyond the trauma of brain cancer by finding what it brought her that she did not have before. Perhaps that is why she seemed proud of her life-threatening experience.

She also reminded me to say that trauma can leave physical as well as emotional or psychological scars. This artist might be able to move beyond the emotional pain of her ordeal with cancer, but she was resigned to living with the physical scars in her brain that had robbed her of being able to hear on the left side. A young man I worked with 15 years ago also had psychological as well as physical scars from his trauma. As a baby he was physically beaten by an abusive parent. His head took the brunt of the abuse and the tragic result was paralysis on his right side. Both these individuals were not only struggling with healing and moving on from the psychological aftermath of the traumatic experience, but they also had physical effects that they could not move beyond regardless of their motivation. But even with the tragedy of brain cancer in such a young woman, she was able to focus her attention on the positive aspects of the physical scars.

The First Rule of Helpers—Do No Harm

To the degree that the healing professions of psychology, medicine and social work have encouraged traumatized individuals to define themselves as survivors, we need to take responsibility for this and change the way we work with this issue. In the same way, the support system of a person who has been traumatized needs to continue to see the individual's hopes and dreams before the trauma and not accept a scaled down version of the person simply due to a very bad experience. We must all agree that we must first do no further harm to the individual.

It is easy to see how one could do active harm to a trauma survivor. To a child who had a near drowning experience and was afraid of the water, it is not a good idea to throw them into the deep end of the pool to have them get over their fear, with an approach of sink or swim. There are people who think this way, but it is insensitive and can cause further harm. But we can also do harm by standing by and letting the negative consequences of trauma solidify into an unhappy life for the person. This would result in more of a victim than a survivor. I think that trauma survivors need to know from those of us who support them that their lives can go forward, their dreams can be realized, and that when they change in unnecessary ways from trauma, this gives the experience more power to cause damage.

THE PATH TO HEALING

Avoid letting the trauma define you.

Since trauma is about losing power, then use your internal power to redefine the experience.

The goal is to have power over the experience, rather than let the experience have power over you.

True power is deciding how much relevance you decide to give an experience.

When trauma happens, let yourself express what is real, be patient and caring to yourself, ask for support from others, seek professional help if you wish, put the experience into words, thoughts and feelings, heal as long as necessary, then move on.

Do not trade your dreams for the title of survivor.

Rely on your support system.

FOUR

LIFE, LIBERTY, AND THE PURSUIT OF UNHAPPINESS

After a recent national election, experts were discussing the role the constitutional issues played in decisions by voters. One of the experts made a fascinating observation. He asked the question "if our founding fathers returned today and saw the results of their efforts 230 years later, what would they think?" Part of his answer was that most of them would be very surprised that our country had made the constitution into a quasi-religious dogma to be respected, preserved and defended as written. He went on to say that the framers of the constitution were attempting to provide a living document — one that would be changed and altered over time, something the rigid monarchies and inflexible laws of tradition did not do.

In line with this question of what the founders would think, I wonder how they would view what we have done with the building blocks of human rights outlined in the Declaration of Independence as the right to life, liberty, and the pursuit of happiness. I wonder if a Thomas Jefferson would not read with enthusiasm the work of psychology and our understanding of the brain and its role in health and happiness, and then wonder why we are ignoring the truths that are so self-evident.

Regarding our inalienable right to life and liberty, I believe he would notice with excitement the advances in medicine that have allowed us to nearly double our life expectancy over the last 230 years. I think he would be pleased with the move away from slavery in which he participated, but with which he was never comfortable. I think he would at the same time be dismayed with the evidence throughout our country that the value of life is not held more sacred than it is. I believe he would notice our fascination with death, violence, and crime that pervades our news and entertainment. He might point out that our federal government has come dangerously close to limiting our civil rights at home and threatening international rights abroad. I believe he might possibly point out that when the United States was founded, we were fighting the arrogant influence of the world's most powerful nation, both economically and militarily. It would not surprise me if he observed that the tables had turned as now many countries in the world view our President George in much the same way our founders viewed King George.

But I believe he might save his most stinging criticism for what we have done with the opportunities earned for us by our founding fathers to pursue happiness[1] in our lives, our homes and our communities. Would he not find that we are looking in all the wrong places for happiness? No doubt he would be amazed with our technological advances, but would he find that these have brought more happiness into

---

1. *Some historians believe the term happiness in the Declaration of Independence was meant to indicate financial or vocational pursuits. While this has some validity, I believe Thomas Jefferson had a broader meaning of happiness. The founders of our nation knew the type of government they wished to establish — one that provided inalienable rights to ideas and opinions, to speaking freely, to freedom of travel and other pursuits that did not infringe on the rights of others. In addition, they wished to found a government that ensured freedom of belief, of faith, and of religion. Thus the inalienable rights were to be construed to include pursuit of vocational interests as well as personal pursuits of self-determination related to mind, body and spirit.*

our lives? He would no doubt marvel at the educational opportunities that abound in modern America, but has our educational level made us a wiser and happier nation? The capitalistic economic system that had its birth in the early days of our country would impress Mr. Jefferson, but with the increased standard of living would he find a commensurate increase in life satisfaction and happiness? I believe the answer to each of these questions would be a surprising or even shocking no. In fact, he might notice our standard of living going up and our satisfaction with our lives going down. If there is any truth to this, what is at play in this odd dynamic?

Perhaps more so in our culture of abundance than other cultures, there appears to be what I would call a happiness fallacy. This comes from the belief that if we get what we want, the achievement itself will make us happy. We are told throughout life to strive for more, to set our sights high, and not to be satisfied with less than reaching the stars. This may be somewhat overstated, but in our society children are not guided toward being laborers, assembly-line workers, or low level bureaucrats. However, much of the American workforce is made up of such positions. Children are encouraged to have lofty goals, which is good. But children are not taught that simply achieving something does not guarantee happiness or personal contentment. In fact, our modern economic machine does not look kindly on the individual who is satisfied with the status quo. Unlike many cultures in the world that have a better sense of what brings happiness, our culture holds out achievement, status, advancement, and upward mobility as the goal and assumed route to happiness. However, for most Americans achievement often becomes the pursuit of unhappiness.

ॐॐ

We're number one! We're number one!

This familiar chant at sporting events is often repeated in our culture that values being the first at anything and everything. Let's consider what we are number one in: billionaires, Olympic medals in 2004, internet users, Nobel prize winners, roads, airports, the economic size, and gold reserves. That sounds fine, but what else? The US is also number one in: military stationed in other countries, citizens in jail, military spending, nuclear weapons, crimes against children, arms sales, energy consumption, and the largest national debt in the world. For health care we spend more per person than any nation in the world, but we lag behind many nations in health categories, and we are losing ground each year. Where are we not even close to being number one? Happiness! Too bad we can't buy happiness or we would be number one there as well (Wallechinsky, 2007).

∂∾∽

The fundamental problem with happiness in our culture is that it is one of the few things that cannot be bought regardless of the price. Happiness cannot be acquired through any level of achievement or advancement in our standard of living. Happiness is not bestowed upon us by awards, promotions, praise or the respect of others. Happiness is not about what goes on outside of us, but what goes on inside.

But isn't this talk heresy to our American beliefs? Isn't wealth better than poverty? Isn't career advancement better than being overlooked for promotions? Aren't beauty, power, influence, and the respect of others the stuff of personal contentment? Unfortunately, there are too many

examples that point out all the above are a part of the
happiness fallacy. Whether we strive to be as desirable as
Marilyn Monroe, as powerful as Richard Nixon, as
influential as Kenneth Lay, or as wealthy as the most recent
lottery winner, none of this will bring us happiness. Unlike
the promise of achievement connected to the happiness
fallacy, happiness cannot be acquired or achieved from the
outside.

It is true that wealth is generally better than poverty,
but it turns out that having enough money and resources
brings more happiness than wealth brings. It is true that
achieving our personal goals can bring happiness, although
not because others offer us respect or praise, but rather
internally because we are deserving of respect and praise.
The advertising industry would like you to believe that
happiness is obtainable through whiter teeth, more
fashionable clothing, or the right car. This should not
surprise us. What should surprise us is the number of
people who live their lives indicating that they believe the
fallacy that any exterior change will bring with it an internal
state of contentment and happiness.

I use a variety of methods to teach the children I work
with the "secrets" to a good life. I use the word secret to
describe important lessons leading to success because
children like fun secrets. When I tell them a secret to being
happy, the children hear this as something others don't
have access to and that is, therefore, special. This principle
apparently works with adults as well, as shown in the
marketing of the book *The Secret* (Bryne, 2007). There are
many secrets to a good life, but one of the most important is
that we get the most when we give the most. To get this
message across, I enjoy telling the children I work with that
I am wealthy. Most children, particularly those who have
had little in life, are intrigued with wealth. In fact, I tell these
children that I am the wealthiest person in the world. Of
course, I am referring not to money, but to the fact that

because of what I give to others I get back more than I give, as well as personal satisfaction and meaning and purpose in my life. Recently one of the children in a group challenged me by saying, "You are not the world's wealthiest man, Bill Gates is." I responded, "Not so, just last week (this was mostly true) Bill Gates found out that I was the wealthiest man in the world, and he quit the highest paying job on the planet to give money away full time to become as wealthy as I am." The young man had no comeback. Just the week before this conversation Bill Gates had announced that he was stepping down as the CEO of Microsoft to work with his foundation. However, there is some doubt as to whether he did this to compete with me.

I think I was able to convey to the children the idea that money will not bring happiness, at least not acquiring more money than one needs. This is an important lesson often missed by those in all age groups, including corporate executives. I believe the children can understand that being famous, although a goal of many in our culture, does not bring happiness with it either. Power, influence, and material things may be an aspect of our personal goals, but none guarantees happiness. I believe that even the young children with whom I talk can understand this when explained, so why is our culture in apparent hot pursuit of unhappiness?

Happiness Is an Inside Job, Start to Finish

I usually avoid using the term happiness because it has different meanings to different people. There are at least two types of happiness to which we commonly make reference. The first is the state of being happy that comes from something that produces short-term pleasure. This could also be called gratification. We watch our child in the school play and this makes us happy. It does not help with our demanding boss the next day, but right after our child does his or her best in the play, we have a special feeling inside that is hard to beat. We also say that our new car, a fine glass of wine with a special meal, when our team wins the big game, and other similar short-term states bring us a brief degree of happiness.

The other type is long-term happiness. This is not particularly connected to gratification and has much more to do with how we live our lives. It is more related to internal contentment over time than having things go our way momentarily. Either type of happiness is an inside experience of being pleased, either briefly or chronically.

We would all love to be chronically pleased and happy. However, our society has such a skewed sense of the meaning of happiness that we confuse the state of being with the object that produces the state. We are taught through our consumer society to equate happiness with things, with accomplishments, with external approval or rewards. For example, the actress is happy to be honored with the Golden Globe or Oscar. But it is entirely possible that the award was more of a popularity contest and the competing actresses know this. It is not always our most gifted actors who win the awards but those who most of their peers want to honor, which is a very different thing. It makes sense to me that the entertainment industry, with its focus on image and recognition, has the highest number of awards of every kind (Tony, Grammy, Emmy, SAG, Oscar, Golden Globe, People's Choice, CMA, to mention just a few). I am trying to imagine multiple awards programs each year honoring the top nominated plumbers or perhaps dentists. "In this year's award for best root canal are the following nominees..." It is possible to be nominated and not win or to win and not feel like you deserve it; both could bring a special type of unhappiness along with those who were not recognized at all. True happiness comes from self-recognition, not from the fickle whims of popularity outside of us.

When we equate our internal state of being with what happened outside of us that elicited this state, we fundamentally confuse the concept of happiness. There is nothing wrong with gratification, pleasure, and good things coming our way in life, and most of us receive at least short-term happiness when this occurs. Yet we need to understand that the state of happiness is within us, and we allow it to see the light of day when we choose to do so, with external events playing only a supporting role. Could a person in jail experience happiness? Absolutely yes. Could someone who has achieved wealth, power, and recognition still not find the state of happiness? Without question. In fact, the Bible says it is easier for a camel to go through the eye of a needle than to have a rich man enter the kingdom of heaven. A true state of happiness may be more difficult for someone who's goal is acquisition, accomplishment, and gain. This is due to the fact that happiness requires the conceptual understanding of sufficiency. How much power is enough, how much wealth is enough, and how much name recognition and praise from others is sufficient?

Long-term happiness, despite what we are told from Madison Avenue, has little connection with external factors. We either chose to live in a world that feeds our spirit, or we look for something else that will do it for us. Short-term gratification and pleasure come from the immediate state of having something good happen, anything from a chocolate bar to an unexpected salary increase. However, long-term happiness requires satisfaction coming from within rather than something that splashes on us from the outside. As much as we like to hang onto the short-term high, it will always elude us like the child who blows beautiful bubbles but must blow more and more because they do not stay around long. Too many people in our culture live their lives groping for the beautiful bubbles that we can surely count on to make us happy: money, possessions, the perfect Pinot Noir, or the ideal sexual partner.

How the Pursuit of Unhappiness Can Affect Traumatized Individuals

As much as the pursuit of happiness through gratification, recognition, power, and acquisition of material things affects so many people, it has a particular impact on people who have been through significant trauma. When traumatized people who struggle in life, as well as all dissatisfied individuals, look around, they see happy people everywhere. This is similar to someone who has lost a partner, and immediately notices all the couples at restaurants and at the mall. Unhappy people believe that nearly everyone else is better off than they are, and the rest of the world is having fun while they are depressed. Not all people who have gone through trauma are depressed and desperately unhappy, but a higher percentage are than in the non-traumatized population.

The first struggle for those who has been through something very difficult in life and who have lingering emotional after affects, is they often believe that they are alone in their pain. From the position of a hungry person, everyone else can look well-fed. Although this is not accurate, it is difficult for the traumatized individual to understand that the struggle to find happiness is as real for others as it is for him or her. It appears to be an aspect of the human condition to believe that everyone else has what we cannot seem to obtain.

For many people, but particularly for traumatized individuals, the tendency is to develop an "if only" orientation to life. I would have had a good life if only I was not sexually abused. I would have gotten that promotion if only I had been treated fairly. I would be happy if only…(fill in the blank). We can all find ourselves stuck in "if only" thinking. The truth is often that events in life can increase our struggle for what we want, but seldom can these events take away our inner satisfaction unless we hand it over willingly.

Traumatized individuals can convince themselves that it just isn't possible to be content with a life that has brought them such pain. If the person keeps thinking this, it will likely become the person's reality. At the same time, those who fight this type of thinking can regain the initial control they had of what they choose to think, what they choose to feel, and internally decide how they view their life. It is difficult for a traumatized person to avoid the trap of negative thinking, but in this respect the person shares this struggle with everyone on the planet, including those with wealth, power, and recognition by others.

Falling Short of Our Inalienable Rights

Much of our society has confused long-term happiness with pleasure and gratification. It is not a surprise that our country's rates of alcohol use, drug use, and sexual fixation are some of the highest on the planet. Nicotine, alcohol and caffeine are used as crutches to help us achieve a state that we would like to be in, but we do not take the time or learn how to get there without the external fix. We can get high on seeing a sunset, but this is not as sure a thing as a good stiff drink. So our collective confusion as to what happiness is comes out culturally when we believe that "life, liberty, and the pursuit of happiness" has to do with being able to do whatever we want to do. This was never the intended meaning.

When we pursue gratification we eventually have to come down, and there is always some disappointment when coming down from the pleasure. On our most wonderful vacations we have to return home and back to daily life; after the party of the year we must wash the dishes and clean up the house. However, if we understand pursuit of happiness to mean long-term happiness, then we know that we have the opportunity to find real meaning for ourselves — to learn how to live in the state of happiness when things are good and when they are not so good. Everyone's life has periods of both ups and downs, and we cannot always order the kind of day we would like in the way we can go to Burger King and have it our way. Until we as individuals, and collectively as a culture, learn about long-term happiness, we will be running in a well-worn circle after the next short-term high that we believe will bring us happiness.

Over the last few years I have been increasingly aware of how often the media reports that the United States is slipping in some measure of dominance in the world. We have fallen behind Asia in manufacturing. We have fewer Nobel Prize winners than in the past. To everyone's embarrassment, our Olympic basketball "Dream Team" has not been #1 in the last few tournaments. I find myself wondering why the United States has to lead the world in productivity, math scores, exports, and most everything else that we can measure. Can we handle being number two or even number twelve? Is our national self-confidence so shaky that we must be first in everything? This seems like a game of "mine is bigger than yours." I can't help but believe this is related to the collective misunderstanding of what happiness really is.

Thirty years ago our excuse for excessive com-petitiveness was that the communists would rule the world if we did not beat them to it. Did anyone else notice that after the collapse of the Soviet Union, other than a gloating smile from the Western world, life didn't change much? It seemed like we picked some new enemies and villains and life went on. In a sense, we now have an even more sinister enemy than communists that justifies our vigilance and reactivity, and the new enemy is the shadowy global terrorist. This is not to discount any real threat, but was Communism ever the threat described by Joseph McCarthy or even Ronald Reagan? Today, can we distinguish between the real threats in the world and our fears and reactivity?

There are many measures that show the United States today is more powerful, influential, and has more resources than any nation in the world—but has this brought us happiness? The race for outer space, the clash with socialism, and the constant pressure for America to be on top has brought us little societal happiness. Any sports team that has climbed the ladder of success and won the World Series, the Stanley Cup, or the Super Bowl, learns that if winning is the only goal, when you are on top there is only one direction to go, and that is down.

For the person who has experienced trauma and strives to move beyond the experience and reach personal contentment, he or she will have to understand the difference between short-term gratification and long-term happiness.

How We Learn about Happiness

Like everything else in life, children learn about happiness by observing the modeling of the adults around them and learning from the environment. The powerful influence of modeling can be shown in a couple of examples. If we made a list of the things that most children could not live without, at least in their own minds, the list would surely include TV, sugar, toys, and much more. Let's take a look at the first two. In the treatment programs I have run for many years, we have never had television available. TV has become the great babysitter in many families where parents only have time to themselves if the child is asleep or in front of the tube. This is even more true for children who have emotional and/or behavioral problems. Most of the children who come into our treatment programs have had the daily average exposure to TV in America, which most recently is six to seven hours or more per day (yes, you read that right). We have no television in our programs because of many reasons—including the problem with a child watching life rather than directly experiencing life, as well as the generally negative influences of advertising, violence, and for young children the questionable moral content of some programs. However, even with children who have been raised on television, every child who has come into our programs forgets about vicarious living through TV after only a day or two. After they leave our program some go back to television addiction, but many say they no longer have interest in TV. Rather they prefer activities, hobbies, or reading instead.

The second basic need a child will tell you they have is sugar. In our treatment programs we have eliminated the excessive empty calories and absent nutritional value of sugar in a child's diet. Some sugar sneaks in, such as in a birthday cake, but the sugar in most processed foods is not found in our programs. One family contacted me after a child left our program to say, "What did you do to her? She no longer likes sweet things." The power of example and learning from the environment is substantial in children.

In the same way, children observe what pleases a parent and what makes the most important people in their lives happy. In less than stellar homes, we have had children become so aware of what pleases a parent that they learn how to get dad another beer, or mix a drink for mom. They will bring a parent a pack of cigarettes or even take drugs with parents to give them company. Other families enjoy talking together during family dinners, taking family trips to the beach or to play in the snow, or spending positive time in many other ways. Whether it is sitting in front of the TV for hours because a parent does, or having family game night once a week, children always pick up information about what makes the adults around them happy.

Most adults will tell a child that happiness is all about being with those you love, helping others, having what you need and sharing what you have, and many other pleasant-sounding sentiments. But does the child see these things in daily living in the family? Like any other concept in life, happiness is not learned by listening to the words of adults. Children learn happiness by living and observing the examples all around them. Do the children of smokers have a higher likelihood of smoking themselves? Yes. Are children of hunters more likely to be hunters? Yes. Do children of families that are a part of a positive faith community more often pursue such support as adults? Yes. It is important that we are aware of what we are teaching our children about happiness by the way we live our lives.

What is the message we learn about happiness as we grow up from modeling, verbal messages, media, and all other sources? Certainly there are some different messages that children learn, depending on the environment they grow up in. But overall, our culture puts a great deal of emphasis on happiness. Some people believe that our society produces more happiness due to our constitutional republic, our bill of rights, our system of laws, and our protection of the individual from the state. However, it would be difficult to support this position with facts from other cultures. It may be that our society talks more about happiness than others, but we are not the happiest people on the planet—despite being the first country to have Disneyland, the self-proclaimed "happiest place on earth."

In our society we view happiness as being directly related to our freedom. We have a long tradition of a "live free or die" mentality. It is hard for us to imagine people being happy in a country that is being subjugated by another country because our nation was founded in opposition to tyranny. We also equate happiness with abundance and having what we need, and more if at all possible. We value security, particularly financial security. In our service-based economy, planning, tracking, counting, exchanging, auditing, and disbursing money are all essential aspects of modern living, and all are held out to us as potentially adding to our happiness.

We value being influential in America. We expect important people or those who set trends, make decisions, or do something that other people look up to, to be happier than the rest of us. In part this comes from watching how much effort the politician, athlete, recording artist and others must put into their careers before they hit the big time. Once there, they must feel like they are on top of the world.

Our society also holds up career development and success as adding to happiness in life. In a competitive world like ours, getting ahead often can mean beating someone else to the goal. Everyone does not win the race, so getting ahead can be at the expense of others falling back. With success, resources, freedom, and power to influence all strongly linked with our sense of happiness, we have created some problems. Although there is an internal component to these issues, they are fundamentally external to the individual. The athlete who wins the game but did not do her best is often happier than the athlete with the best performance of her life, but in a losing effort.

Having enough money is seldom linked to happiness, because how much is enough? We believe that significant amounts of money and not adequate amounts will make us happy. We would be quick to fight a war to protect our freedom to vote, but a surprisingly low number of eligible voters actually participate in elections in this country. The problem is that many aspects of what we believe are related to happiness are not. External gain and achievement appear to have little to do with internal happiness.

Those who have lived through trauma such as child abuse and neglect must identify what kind of modeling they received related to happiness. Unless you consider what is present in your internal thinking about happiness, you might gravitate to the pursuits of the adults who modeled for you early in life. This may not serve you well. It is worth taking an inventory of your beliefs about short and long-term happiness. Do you believe it is within your grasp? What does happiness look like for you? Are you clear that it will not come from external sources? It may be a good idea for everyone to consider such questions, but if you had poor early modeling of how to achieve life satisfaction and happiness, these questions are critical.

Looking for Love in All the Wrong Places

If we have in our society a faulty sense of what happiness is, it is not surprising that we could live in a country that excels in all external areas but does not lead the world in personal contentment. How is it that the good old days are actually now, but most people mistakenly believe that times were better in the past? Perhaps the answer is that we have been looking for what we all want, personal contentment and happiness, in all the wrong places.

It is true that people with financial resources are more satisfied with life overall than those with little or no resources. However, it is not true that people with massive amounts of wealth are happier than people with limited but adequate financial resources. We know that influence and power does not always bring contentment—as we watch what power does to people. Fame is not a guarantee of happiness regardless of how much the individual worked for it. Many famous people would do anything to regain some anonymity.

ॐ

Epicurus had helpful insight 2,300 years ago

The Greek philosopher Epicurus lived in 300 BC, but he had very developed ideas on happiness. He wrote many books, but none survived. We know of his philosophy from writings carved in stone tablets. Epicurus believed that happiness was the end result of friends, freedom, and an analyzed life. He said friends were critical to being happy, and current research agrees. He stressed freedom not only from slavery or subjugation, but also freedom from false needs, things we believe we must have but do not really need. There is much wisdom in this second point as well. Madison Avenue survives on convincing us our wants are needs, but happiness does not come with the transaction. He believed that we must analyze our life to be happy. Most philosophers would agree that thoughtful consideration of our lives does make us different than all other living creatures on the planet. Whether it makes you happy to consider your life depends on what you see, and what you do with what you find. Epicurus valued pleasure, but to him this was the richness and wonder of the human senses. He had a following who lived very simply from a material standpoint, but valued non-material wealth. Epicurus was very close to understanding happiness so many years ago. It is somewhat ironic that his name is used today in the word epicurean, meaning the pursuit of sensual pleasures and delights such as fine food, wine, luxury and sexual pursuits. Epicurus knew happiness was more than this, but over time people only remembered what they wanted from his ideas.

☙❧

Perhaps the greatest deception in our society is the major role played by advertising to teach us what we need to be content and happy in our lives. After convincing us of our need, they then offer the solution in just three easy payments. With the right hair products, the right vehicle, the right look, the right phone, and the right health plan, how are we going to handle all the happiness we are promised? Clearly we do not struggle with too much contentment in America. Instead, as our lives seem to improve, our net worth increases, and our share of the American dream comes our way, we struggle with finding ourselves much less fulfilled and happy than we were hoping. We also find much less satisfaction than we were promised by a society that pretends to offer happiness from the outside.

What Is Wrong With Money, Power, and External Success?

There are many obvious fallacies in some of our society's views of personal contentment. The first we have stated several times: contentment does not come from outside us, but from within us. No amount of money or power or influence or career success will guarantee personal contentment. When we consider money, power and success, none of these are the problem in themselves. The problem is that they just do not provide what we often hope they will. There is no question that we can be a happy captain or a miserable general, a content teacher or a discontented principal, a satisfied section supervisor or a dissatisfied president of the company. It is what is inside each of these people that makes the difference.

There is nothing inherently wrong with money, power or success. Most people in our culture are striving for these and other signs that they are high achievers in life. But if any or all of these come in abundance, I think the promise of what they bring and what actually is delivered is very problematic. Many good people are corrupted by these measures of achievement. I happen to believe that most corporate executives do not climb the corporate ladder hoping to one day take over the company and lie, cheat and steal from as many shareholders as possible. Even the famous examples of corporate greed that are all too common these days most likely involve good people who began with good intentions but were corrupted with the false promise that more is always better.

If our modern belief about happiness was put into an honest straightforward bumper sticker, I think it would say "More Is Better." But there is ample evidence that this is just not true. Let me use a family example here. My father served a long and distinguished career in the United States Air Force and retired to start a second career as a financial advisor. I learned many very important financial lessons from him. I have made good financial decisions, and I have many opportunities because of good planning and disciplined financial behavior. I owe much of this successful part of my life to my father and his financial lessons and wisdom. There is one thing I did not learn from my father when it came to money that I believe is critically important. I did not learn from him how much was enough.

I did not learn this lesson from my father because I believe this was a lesson that his life experience did not teach him. Life in the Great Depression, and the ups and downs over the many decades he lived, did not leave much room to consider when one's possessions were enough. If he had more, there was always more that could be achieved. So my father was unable to pass this lesson on to me because he did not learn that lesson in his life. It is a wisdom that I do not find in our capitalistic system or in the corporate world. How could any business executive believe that he or she is worth a $5, $50, or $100 million salary to a company and its clients or shareholders? My answer is that these people compare themselves with others and find nothing unfair about it. However, looking deeper, this businessperson could quickly find that, although he or she oversees people working very hard and doing essential functions for the company, these essential workers are paid 1/50th, 1/300th, or even 1/3,000th as much as the top executive is paid. I believe this stems from the lack of understanding by these executives and our corporate world of the answer to how much is enough.

If we want to be happy, we must answer this question and change our national bumper sticker from "More is better" to "Enough Is Just Right." Knowing how much is enough, whether it concerns money, power, success or any other achievement we value in our society, is one key to personal contentment. Before moving on from this topic, I want to focus a bit more on our national perceptions of how much is enough, and how our societal attitudes are reflected in our internal success rather than our external success.

The Paradox of Prosperity—As We Grow Richer, We Seem to Get Poorer

In the recent book *The Progress Paradox*, Gregg Easterbrook makes a compelling point that by nearly every measure, the good old days are now. However, prosperity has not brought with it the happiness that was expected (Easterbrook, 2003). Easterbrook points out that the generally held belief that times were better in the past is not supported by the data. He also makes the case that the belief that American society is in steady decline is not supported by evidence. At the same time that resources, health, education, safety, standard of living, crime rates, the environment, intelligence levels, and global economics are all getting better, most men and women feel less happiness in their lives than was the case in previous generations.

When beliefs contradict facts, we tend to look outside of ourselves for the explanation. It must be that opportunities in recent times are not as great as in previous generations. Not according to the evidence. Because we are not as happy as Americans have been in the past, this must be because we live in a world that has less safety and security. But again this is not supported by the facts. No Virginia, you are less happy because of something inside of you, not because of what is outside of you.

Easterbrook's book thoroughly review why Americans today are not as happy as Americans of the past, although the rise in prosperity is evident. I want to add a couple thoughts related to trauma. The first point is related to what we have discussed about looking outside of us for happiness. Nearly everyone on the planet would say that winning a million-dollar lottery would bring with it long-term possibilities and therefore happiness, but they would be wrong in most cases. Our societal mistake to pursue happiness in consumption, gratification, pleasure, acquisition and improved standard of living is evident here. Each of these desires can be positive, but they do not equate to the internal state of happiness. We must look within if happiness is the real goal.

There is another factor I believe is involved in the paradox of prosperity. Psychology has developed a new understanding of trauma that is not directly experienced but affects us just the same. This is vicarious trauma. Briefly stated, this is when we have a trauma response to events that occur to others and we experience the events second-hand. On the family farm in the 30s and 40s life was hard, opportunities were much more restricted than we have today, and every standard of living was lower. On the farm bad things happened. Death often came early to animals and family and friends. But the frequency of traumatic events that came to daily awareness was a fraction of what it is today thanks to mass communication. We have double the population on the planet as we did just half a century ago, and we now have access to every major traumatic event in the world. This means there are many more of us to experience catastrophic events, as the information is available everywhere we turn. We know when a giant wave hits Indonesia, and we hear about the commercial plane crash that occurs somewhere in the world every few days. We know about the mother who intentionally drowns her five children and many other horrible events that leave a mark on our perception of safety and security, two necessary components for happiness.

Vicarious traumatization to some degree happens to all of us for no other reason than we have the modern day challenge of handling very bad news constantly. We could return to the information absence of the old days, but it would take a great deal of effort. We would have to not read the newspaper, listen to the radio, get on the internet, watch TV, or speak to others who do any of these. It would appear that we are stuck with constant exposure to the worst experiences that happen anywhere on the planet. Unless we realize that bad things have always happened to human beings, we will not be able to put our current exposure into context. Wars in Iraq, Afghanistan, Lebanon, Sudan, among other trouble spots in the world, do not indicate that our planet today has more military conflict than in the 1940s or nearly any other time in history.

Vicarious traumatization is challenging to everyone, but particularly to someone with a history of trauma. We must understand our internal response to seeing a serious accident on the freeway, hearing about an acquaintance having a fatal heart attack, and learning of the latest rapes, murders and tortures in the news. How do we handle all this and not believe that our country and our world are going downhill rapidly? There are no easy answers to this question, but we must start with understanding the effects of things that happen to us, including vicarious things. I believe collectively vicarious traumatization has influenced the societal sense of safety, security, and, ultimately, happiness.

Keeping Our Eye on the Prize

Although there is some evidence that people across cultures are preset to be happy (Diener & Diener, 1995), the sociological evidence appears to be that we must now work harder at being happy than in the past. If we lived up to the intentions of the founders of the United States and truly pursued happiness, just what would this mean? Primarily it would mean that we buck the American belief that happiness is what we feel when things go well for us. As we have discussed, pleasure, advancement, and other good things give us short-term gratification, but they do little for the lasting sense of contentment most of us desire. If we find true happiness, there is evidence that we may well find success in life as well (Lyubomirsky, S., King, L. & Diener, E., 2006). In order to live in a state of contentment we must know what long-term happiness is and where it comes from, and put in the effort to achieve this internal state. Briefly stated, we must get and keep our eye on the prize.

The evidence of declining satisfaction with life, at the same time we are reaching many of our external hopes and dreams, points out the challenge for all of us. Those of us who have experienced trauma of any kind must work even harder. This is not fair, but this is what is real. Regardless of what the trauma is, unless the person heals and moves on, frequent invitations will be provided to re-experience the situation all over again. Crime, child abuse, violence, accidents, burning houses, floods, sudden deaths—these are what our society considers news. Unless you want your brain's limbic system to send you through your own trauma once again, you must do more to heal than someone who is cut-off from the constant barrage of news and information. Just as a person must move beyond the screaming internal challenges of trauma, that person must move beyond the external reminders that all around us there is trauma as well. If we do not, happiness will elude us as it does many of our fellow citizens who unknowingly are busy in the pursuit of unhappiness.

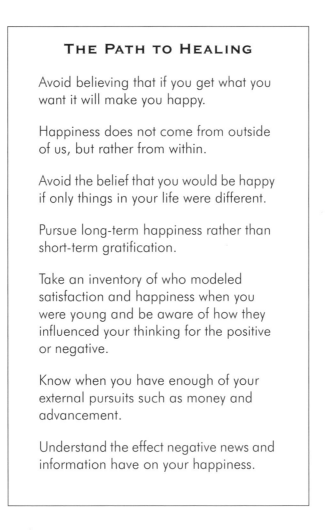

THE PATH TO HEALING

Avoid believing that if you get what you want it will make you happy.

Happiness does not come from outside of us, but rather from within.

Avoid the belief that you would be happy if only things in your life were different.

Pursue long-term happiness rather than short-term gratification.

Take an inventory of who modeled satisfaction and happiness when you were young and be aware of how they influenced your thinking for the positive or negative.

Know when you have enough of your external pursuits such as money and advancement.

Understand the effect negative news and information have on your happiness.

FIVE

RESILIENCY

When bad things happen in life they can have a significant impact on an individual. At times we can handle such a situation and at others times the situation handles us. We have already discussed a wide variety of traumatic experiences from which it is very difficult to recover emotionally. We must even contend with how our pre-set brains ensure that we remember traumatic experiences in a serious and lasting way. Life is full of bad experiences, and if we allow any of these to overwhelm us, the results can be devastating to our dreams and hamper our experience of happiness in life. When bad things happen to us, our job is to bounce back from the experience as much as possible. The concept of resiliency deserves some specific focus here, because this is the meaning of being resilient: to bounce back from adversity.

What Is Resiliency and Why Is It So Important?

There are many difficult things that come with living. It has been said that birth and death are both painful events, as is much of life in between. With traumatic experiences part of the human condition, we all are faced with the challenge of bouncing back when bad things happen to us. In some ways, we have not lived a full life without adversity.

Traumatic events come in a variety of forms. They can be caused by external forces such as natural disasters or accidents. They can also be caused by the actions of others such a physical or sexual assault or child abuse. Traumas by their nature are beyond our control. I now want to consider how we learn from childhood to adapt to difficult events in life. If positive adaptations were not learned in childhood, it is not too late to learn to not only survive but thrive in the face of adversity.

There is a familiar saying that if we do not learn from history then we are doomed to repeat it. This statement points out the importance of learning from our past experiences both as individuals and as a society. It would be great if we learned all we needed to know about living from sanitized sources such as advice from parents, lessons in school, or libraries. But when a parent assures the young teen that his young girlfriend breaking up with him is not the end of the world, such reassurance falls on deaf ears in the face of such a devastating life experience. If we could completely learn our lessons from others and not have to make the same mistakes, we could save ourselves many serious problems. But if we went back in time, we would likely find that the person now teaching was not listening when he or she was young and had to learn these lessons by experience. This leads us to the question, is learning about life really possible from the experience of others rather than our own experiences?

It would seem that there are some lessons that can and must be learned from others. Our parents tell us about running into the street or riding a bike in front of an oncoming vehicle. I remember being seven and riding my bike after school in front of my house. I came down my sloped driveway and into the street directly in front of a car. The driver slammed on his brakes, barely stopping before hitting me. I was untouched and was surprised by the intense anger of the driver as he yelled at me for causing this near catastrophe. I did not understand his intensity at the time; I could stop my bike, he could stop his car, nothing happened, so why the anger? When my parents used the experience to help me understand that it is a bad idea to rely on someone else to stop in time to prevent a trip to the hospital or worse, the lesson was combined with the experience, and it stuck. I use this principle every time I get on the road, and so far I feel blessed to have been driving for 40 years without an accident.

It is difficult to imagine the development of wisdom without life experience. As an observer of life, I have noticed that we tend to learn more from negative experiences than positive ones. As the saying goes: "Mistakes are wonderful opportunities to learn." Hopefully, we do learn from our mistakes, but this is not always the case.

There have been some celebrated examples of youth education programs based upon learning from the mistakes of others. However, it appears that this approach is far less effective than hoped. A parent holding a lit cigarette while telling the child to never smoke, will likely not be listened to due to the influence of modeling behavior. Drug programs have been set up to have addicts share with children why it is important to "just say no." There are the current federally funded programs to prevent pregnancy and sexually transmitted diseases by abstinence. And there were the "Scared Straight" programs in the 70s where the toughest criminals tried to scare delinquent teens from crime by giving them a taste of prison life. All of these approaches have been shown to have poor to disastrous results. There are a number of reasons why you cannot prevent a young person from making mistakes, but one of them is that we all learn best by our personal experience, not by someone else's words or experiences.

It seems that we need to make mistakes to learn. While we are learning how to negotiate the world in effective ways, we tend to do most everything the wrong way until experience helps us to do it better. This results in our getting a great deal of experience bouncing back from failure. This is where resiliency is critical. Resiliency appears to develop just as success does, first in little things then larger things. It is much easier to bounce back from a small mistake than a major one. One of the essential jobs of a parent is to help a child learn from mistakes while insuring that the magnitude of the mistakes does not pose a threat to the child. For example, we tell young children not to run into the street, but we do not give them the option of finding out for themselves why we teach this. We also talk to children about the dangers of secret touching with others, particularly an adult, but we do not have them learn from experience why this is important.

As we grow older, the issues of life get more significant and at times much more dangerous. We are learning from experience why it is not a good idea to give 16-year-olds a drivers license before they have developed the maturity of judgment to handle potentially lethal lessons through life experience. I predict that our society will change this law, and when they do a great many teen lives and others on the road will be saved. When we have the responsibility to decide for ourselves where we go, when we come home, how much we drink, whether to smoke, or how to handle sexual expression—the inevitable result is that we will make many mistakes until we get it right (if we ever do get it right). Each time we make large or small mistakes, we either give up or we bounce back. Most of us bounce back to one degree or another, and this requires resiliency.

The importance of resiliency can be seen in the way adults handle stress. Research has found that if there are two groups of adults, one group that has experienced significant trauma and the other that has experienced only the usual challenges of life without significant trauma, the group with the experience of trauma has the better ability to handle stress. Just as the artist who turned her severe damage on her brain's left side into a career relying on her right hemisphere and expressing more creativity, people who have experienced serious trauma can come away from the experience with an advantage in life when facing stress. Of course, this cannot be said of all people who go through traumatic experiences, or traumatized people would be some of our most successful members of society rather than some of the least successful. The distinction is that through resiliency, the individual learned in small and large issues first to bounce back when adversity strikes and second to learn from mistakes. Success in life is based to a large degree on being able to do these two things.

The Resilient Brain

Our brain ensures that we remember some experiences in two separate ways in order to take full advantage of what we can learn to enhance our survival. Trauma is one of those experiences that can be explicitly remembered in the neocortex of the brain and implicitly remembered in the limbic system. The neocortex works to remember important experiences in order to learn from the past to make decisions in the present. This is one of the essential executive functions of the frontal lobes of the brain. The limbic system does not rely on the neocortex because some traumas shut down our explicit memory due to the fact that the situation and its impact on us are too overwhelming. People who experience serious trauma, such as a serious car accident, often remember before and after the accident, but have no conscious memory of the actual collision. At a critical moment the brain shuts down sensory input and decides this is something we had best not consciously remember. To help ensure survival, the limbic system has a separate memory function for traumatic memories that does not rely on conscious recall. Instead, the memory is stored implicitly, meaning it is automatically recalled to help the individual avoid something similar happening in the future.

❧

Lynette could not move beyond her past

My introduction to Lynette was similar to nearly every contact I had with her over the years. She was suspicious, demanding, and she exuded negative energy, not that she didn't have reason to be negative. She had several physical disabilities that structured her life around appointments to doctors of various types. She herself was a medical professional and had very high demands of professionals from whom she sought help, but would say that every one of them let her down. She could no longer hold a job due to her physical disabilities, and to add insult to injury, she had chronic sleep problems. Lynette was a victim of sexual abuse as a child and teen. She was smart and did well in school in all but social areas. Now in her late thirties, she seemed twice her age in all respects. Lynette was a tragic example of how every part of her life had been adversely affected by her traumatic past. Even with disabilities that had her bound to a wheelchair, perhaps the greatest impact of the abuse was on her social relationship. She felt alone even when she was around others. Lynette was consistently unpleasant to me as I supported her in every way I could. She had no friends, no family, and no one in her life, and I could see why. An argument could be made that all aspects of her unfulfilled life could be traced back to her past and how it had been carried into her present. I offered what I could, but it was like pouring water in the desert sands — it was just too little, too late.

❧

The resilient brain in some ways must counteract its own normal operations. It first must work to bring back into conscious memory the events or situation so they can be considered with our higher reasoning. When we recall the past, we perform mental processes such as reviewing the events that led up to the situation, considering whether any steps could have prevented or lessened the impact of the event, reviewing the help that had been asked for and received, and asking if now here are any steps that can be taken as a result.

Depending upon how seriously our coping ability has been compromised by a traumatic event, our brain may first shut down our ability to perform these mental operations. The resilient brain must work to bring as much as possible of the traumatic event back into the conscious mental process in order to take advantage of our considerable ability to achieve mental healing and move on. To shine the light of higher-order reasoning on a situation is one aspect of mental health treatment for traumatic and overwhelming experiences.

The resilient brain must also address the other way the brain naturally responds to overwhelming experiences: through implicit memory. The limbic system cannot rely on the frontal lobes to remember the key element that we do not want to have this experience again, so it sends out an alarm to the body's endocrine, respiratory, circulatory and neurological systems when there is something that is reminiscent of the bad experience. This process can help with survival by reminding the person to avoid high speeds in cars, be very careful in the water, avoid dark alleys in unfamiliar cities, or whatever was involved in the traumatic experience. However, this process can also result in so many false positives (excessively frequent alarm signals when there is no actual threat) that the person's life is adversely affected.

The resilient person must be able to turn on one part of the brain that may have been shut off and to shut off another part of the brain that has been placed on red alert by an overwhelming experience. To do either or both of these steps can be much more difficult than it may sound.

The younger the individual with an overwhelming or traumatic experience, the more vulnerable the person is. This is true because the child's ability to take steps to run away or to fight off the threat is often minimal. Young trauma victims often struggle more because the life experience of the child is limited. Disorientation and fear, based upon the unknown, can amplify the situation to greater levels than if the child had experiences enabling better understanding of what was and was not going on.

Because children more often are overwhelmed with bad things that happen to them, and they are often more adversely affected by events, they will need outside help to be able to train their brains to generate resiliency. This is a major reason why it is a good idea to provide some level of professional mental health care to every child who has experienced trauma. It may be that the support in the child's life has been sufficient to "metabolize" the negative emotions connected to the events, but it is generally a good idea to have at least a quick mental health checkup to consider if there are any lingering issues that may surface later.

If resiliency requires that we turn on one part of our brain and turn off another part, just how do we do this? Both are done somewhat differently because we are working in different directions, finding the on switch in one case and the off switch in the other. Which process is easier and which more difficult will depend upon the individual. It would be my suggestion that a person start with turning on the neocortex frontal lobes as a first step. If this can be successfully done, it will help in the ability to turn off the limbic reactivity.

Our brains are highly suggestible, and we can focus the attention of the brain by our voluntary actions. For example, the main premise behind illusionists or magicians is to tell people's brains to look for something in particular and then to fool the brain. Another example of using the suggestibility of the brain is through hypnosis or auto-suggestion. We tell the brain what to experience, and it obliges and does just that. We can turn the focus of our brains in certain directions, then provide additional information and data and begin to build memories of traumatic events that caused the shut down of explicit memories. Said in a different way, we can reawaken our ability to remember, think about, and give consideration to events that were so traumatic that our reasoning centers were shut down at the time of the event. We can do this by conscious effort, or with the help of a therapist, or by adding factual information from the outside, or by all of the above. The way the brain develops explicit memory is by stimulation of neuron-networks and then making synaptic connections with other networks that remember similar experiences. Through the process of intentionally bringing attention and focus to an event of which we have limited memory, we can build explicit memory that we can then use to enhance our mental process of understanding and healing.

The other step is to work to find the off switch for the alarm that too frequently sounds in the limbic system or specifically in the amygdala, or fear center of the brain. There are many methods to reduce arousal in the brain. There is relaxation, visualization, conscious awareness, thought stopping, thought replacement, cognitive restructuring and other methods. Each of these in some way interrupts the arousal of the reactive part of the brain and brings this reactivity into more conscious control. This is why it may be helpful to first turn on the frontal lobes of the brain where conscious control is enhanced. We can then literally tell ourselves what the limbic system is about to do, and what we will counter with when this occurs.

An example here may be helpful. In a recent talk I was giving I mentioned that if I took out a gun and pulled the trigger right there, everyone would react. Some would scream, some run for the door, some hit the floor, and still others would freeze. All of these reactions would be forms of fight or flight and would have started in the limbic system of the brain. However, if I had everyone relax in the room and I said that I wanted to test everyone's ability to stay calm and told the group I would discharge a gun and to ignore it, the response would be very different. Most likely no one would hit the floor or even come out of their seat. Every person's amygdala would still respond to the sound, but immediately the frontal lobes of the brain would instruct the brain not to react. This process is the goal of working with the over-activated limbic system.

It is unlikely that the limbic system can be trained to the point that it completely shuts off the alarm response associated with past traumatic events. It is more likely that we can anticipate, then cognitively mediate (understand what the alarm is and why it is going off), and then override the reactivity of the cascading hormonal and visceral response of the body to the alarm going off. Another example of this is when someone announces that just after lunch there will be a test of the fire alarm system in the building. It is only a test and people are to go on with their activities. When the alarm sounds, it is definitely noticed by all, and there is an immediate reaction within everyone in the building. But quickly people remember the previous announcement, and one part of the brain gives meaning to the stimuli. This meaning overrides the reactivity of the body to prepare to immediately get out of the building.

With concentrated effort we can have similar success with the limbic alarm sounding when we get in a car following a serious accident. In this situation the neocortex must explain to our limbic system that this is a different experience, all precautions will be taken, and safety will be the primary focus. There will still be an alarm going off, but our executive functions in our frontal lobes will work to override the body's initial reaction to the alarm. With the help of our brain's reasoning centers the body can go on with living and not run from the building during a practice fire alarm or avoid automobiles after a car accident.

Figure 2: The Resiliency Response Cycle

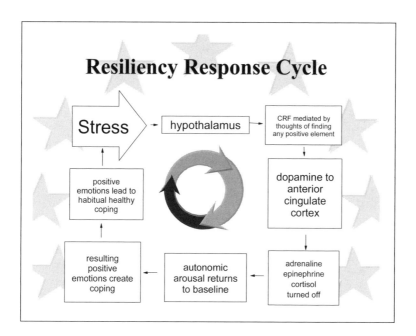

In the first chapter, Figure 1 reflected the stress response cycle. This is one method of depicting what happens within the body when stress begins a process that results in a systemic response. The process just mentioned can also be depicted in such a diagram, which I will refer to as the Resiliency Response Cycle. Figure 2 shows this process. It begins in the same way that the stress response cycle does up to a critical point. Stress is first recorded in the hypothalamus, and its job is to have the body initiate an immediate response to the stress. However, just as in the case of the anticipated fire alarm, the neocortex of the brain mediates or interrupts the normal process. Instead of the cortico tropin stimulating the pituitary and adrenal glands releasing hormones to help the body react to the stress, the frontal lobes provide a different meaning to the alarm and stimulate the release of dopamine to the anterior cingulate cortex. The dopamine interrupts the stress cycle by turning off the release of adrenaline, epinephrine and cortisol, which are designed to enable the body to initiate the fight or flight response. When these hormones are turned off by the influence of the conscious mental process of the higher reasoning center of the brain, the autonomic arousal set-off by the hypothalamus in response to the stress returns to a state of rest or baseline.

But the resiliency cycle is not yet complete, in fact, a very critical process takes place at the point that the body's arousal returns to normal or baseline. The result of the mind's ability to influence the reactivity to the stress produces a sense of control and coping. In a small way, we can experience this when during the practice fire alarm, we ignore the signal to get out of the building and we continue with our activity. We understand the alarm, and we are confident that it can be ignored, and we can cope with the stress involved. In the same way that traumatic experiences that produce the stress response cycle and fight or flight responses are coded in the brain, so also are successful coping responses. When we successfully cope, there are positive emotions that result, and the brain records the fact that we have successfully weathered the stress. This produces an internal sense of growing competence and personal power to respond to stress in an effective way. The more this cycle of coping occurs with small and large stresses in life, the more the brain grows in its recorded memories of positively facing stress — or to use another description, the more resiliency becomes a habitual, healthy coping style.

We May Be What We Eat, but We Definitely Are What We Think

There is a saying that 'you are what you eat.' In the United States we have an abundance of nearly everything and certainly an abundance of food. It is fascinating, and a bit depressing, to consider what we choose to eat. In this country we arguably put more focus on food than any other country. We are not preoccupied with food because of starving populations and famine due to scarcity (although there is definitely hunger in America due to poverty and homelessness); we are focused on food as a nation because it has so much power over us. Go to a bookstore and consider the rows of books with every kind of diet imaginable. Go to a shopping mall and consider the waistlines of the people you pass. Our national girth has been steadily growing since the 1950s. Now go and watch the people stream into the fast food restaurants and see if you notice that the customers are precisely the people who should not be relying on fast food for their nourishment. I believe that with every unhappy meal sold, there should be a small mirror with a statement on top, "You are what you eat, look here to consider the results!" But that would be more difficult to accomplish than the warning labels on cigarette packs.

Due primarily to the diets of Americans, obesity is acknowledged to be a national epidemic. We are now seeing what human beings will choose when there is an unlimited source of every kind of food available all the time. I can walk into a grocery store and buy the same brands of Italian food products that I was excited to find in Rome on a recent visit. We have every kind of fruit every month of the year, not just during local harvest season. There are many brands to choose from regardless of what we are looking for. Unfortunately, this Garden of Eden has not resulted in a well-fed population with a deep sense of gratitude for such abundance. The result is a nation that is obsessed with food as an addiction. We are unhealthy as a society due in part to what we eat, and more concerning are the food choices of our children and the results on their health. Again, I realize that everyone in America is not well-fed, particularly children and the elderly living in poverty, but I am talking about the vast majority of our population.

If we in America are what we eat, the results are cause for concern. We must take responsibility because most of us choose what we eat, and our choices are often less than impressive. But as significant as our diet is on our overall health, the thoughts we choose to fill our minds are even more impactful on who we are. If this sounds like I am saying that we choose our thoughts throughout each day, that is exactly right. Or, I should say that we have the ability to choose our thoughts rather than have other people and situations determine our thoughts for us.

We are definitely what we think. There are countless examples of the power of our thoughts, and being reality-based is not required. For example, from a physical appearance perspective, perhaps the most famously beautiful person in our American history is Marilyn Monroe. Her name was Norma Jean Mortenson before she was transformed in Hollywood to the culturally beautiful Marilyn Monroe. This transformation was in name and appearance only and never became internalized; she spent most of her life believing she was unattractive. The prospect of getting older and losing what little beauty she saw in herself may have contributed to her suicide. Each Christmas season brings traditional songs and among them classics sung by Karen Carpenter. This tragic young woman with a beautiful voice was plagued with anorexia, and though dangerously thin, she believed she was overweight. A third example is a side of Mohandas K. Gandhi that is seldom discussed. One of the most impressive figures in modern history, this man who changed the course of history with his will actually struggled with a type of depression because he believed that he was a failure. In the final years of his life as the world held him in the highest esteem, he had a very dark side of his personality that led him to believe he had been unsuccessful at nearly everything he had done in his life. All of these examples are tragic.

If Norma Jean was ugly, Karen Carpenter was fat, and Gandhi was a failure, the rest of us are in big trouble. But were their self-perceptions accurate? We say "of course not;" they were confused and blinded by their self-doubts. That may be our reality, but their reality was what was important to each of them, just as our reality is what is important to us. And what is our reality of our self? Reality can be a challenging concept because to a very real extent we create reality by our beliefs. In some ways the reality of Monroe, Carpenter and Gandhi were all objectively accurate as their internal reality. That Norma Jean changed her name, hair color, personality, and values and ended up not recognizing who she really was or feeling beautiful in any way makes some sense to me. Gandhi helped open the door to self-rule in the largest democracy in the world, India, and this unleashed decades of just the thing he abhorred—social, political and sectarian violence. So whose perception is the true reality? The answer is more complicated than we like to think.

We do not need to look to the lives of famous or infamous people to find that we are what we think. We simply need to look in the mirror. We are creating our reality every day and every moment. We do this with our choices, with our internal judgments, and with the sensory inputs that come into our brains. We decide if it is a beautiful or ugly day outside. Objective reality would say it is what it is, but we are the ones who use the adjective of our choice to define it. We decide if we had a good day or bad day. Despite the impact of that letter from the IRS, a fight with a friend, or even some bad news from your physician, your day was what it was, and you decided whether you liked or disliked the particulars. There are always some people who would trade their worst day with yours in a heartbeat.

Your thoughts are yours to control unless you give this control away to the people and events in your life. We all are tempted to let external events determine our internal experience, nowhere more than with traumatic experiences. If we let it happen, a single traumatic experience can determine our internal experience for years or even a lifetime. But you cannot let this happen if you seek more than a reactive existence bouncing from one situation to another. Since bad things happen to everyone, the best way to regain control of your internal and external experience is to learn how to recover from problems, failures, and events for which you had no responsibility. The way to exercise this power is through resiliency skills.

Resiliency Skills

Does resiliency come naturally to people, or is it a learned trait? The answer is that resiliency is an instinctual drive in some ways, but it also must be learned in other ways. For example, resiliency at its core is coming back from adversity — when we trip, we get up and continue the journey. On a biological level, life is about resiliency. Our deepest instinct is survival, to prevail against the many forces that work against our survival. Resiliency is keeping at it, putting one foot in front of the other, and biologically, taking that next breath and eating that next meal despite how difficult life may be at the time. The ability to keep going is instinctual, but when we expand our view just a little to include our emotional, psychological and spiritual aspects of life, resiliency must be learned and does not appear to be natural or instinctual.

Despite having our worst day ever, we all expect and rely on our heart to continue to beat and our body to carry us through such a day and into the next day. This is an aspect of being resilient. But after the worst day of our life, or even the worst year ever, we cannot rely on our emotions and our attitudes to be resilient. At times, one very bad event can cause massive negative impacts on our attitude and our emotions for years afterward—we call this a traumatic experience.

If psychological resiliency must be learned, how do we go about this? The best way to learn resiliency skills is from experience. It is one thing to learn a skill in class or read it in a book, but there is no substitute for practice and experience. We could have years of classroom learning and read any number of books, but at some point to be a pilot you must take a plane up off the ground and get the experience of flying. Resiliency is like this. There are books that tell people to give their heart to another person, even though we know that most of the time such a relationship will be temporary and not work out as we initially expect. We read advice to the effect that when we are rejected and our hearts are breaking, we should move on with our lives. Okay, now that I have read this in a book, I have the skill down, and I know what to do when this happens, right? Not so fast; living through it is just a bit different than book learning. Since resiliency is exactly like this, picking yourself up when you fall or when you fail, you will need to live it rather than read it.

We first learn resiliency from example. We see our parents, our teachers, our friends and people we admire go through difficult times and land on their feet with courage and endurance. Or we watch those around us collapse and never get back on the horse after they are bucked off. There are some famous families where resiliency seems to run in their blood line. The Kennedys are such a family. But endurance and courage in the face of adversity are not genetic so much as they are generationally learned by example. The Kennedy clan is known for both tremendous achievement and success along with more than its fair share of difficulties and tragedies.

Before we develop the inner belief in our self, it appears that we need to have the experience of someone else believing in us. Without this happening to us, it is improbable that we will go through life with inner confidence because we never felt the confidence of someone else. This is nothing short of a life-diminishing disaster. When we do have the good fortune of having someone believe in us, there are a number of very important things that we receive. We learn to believe in ourself. I do not think self-belief is natural, I think it initially comes from the outside. We also learn to develop internal confidence from believing in ourself long enough to get better at something with practice and then experiencing some success. Nearly everything we do initially involves failure. This is true of snow skiing, tennis, golf, water skiing, as well as relationships, apologizing, learning math skills and public speaking. Only when we have sufficient confidence to do something despite continual failure or less than optimal performance do we learn to improve and find success with repetition and endurance.

Perhaps the most important resiliency skill is to be able to maintain a positive outlook in the face of difficulty. There are ample reasons in life to get discouraged in the process of learning anything new. Some people do well in difficult situations and others give up immediately. Resiliency is the key factor here, and there are likely to be some predictable elements in the successful person's past that produced the resiliency as well as elements in the past of the person who failed that produced the inability to stand up to adversity.

Resiliency is like a woven fabric. When we look at the whole fabric we see cloth, but if we look closely, we see strands of fabric. The closer we look, the more we see that the whole is carefully woven of individual threads that by themselves look very different than the whole cloth. Resiliency is made up of individual strands of self-confidence, experience of past success, social support, and a positive outlook. When these individual threads are woven together, they form an impressive and strong result.

To come full circle on the issue of resiliency skills, we must come back to the necessity of having someone first believe in us before we learn to believe in ourself. For traumatized individuals, be they children or adults, they will likely need the help of other individuals or a support system that will give them the external belief they need to develop this internally.

Learning Resiliency As Young As Possible

Because we are so dependent upon direct experience to learn skills such as resiliency, the importance of learning such a skill early in life is easy to see. We have discussed the development of what I have referred to as an inner working model. This view of the world also is an inner view of ourself. Some children develop a sense that they can do no wrong, or they can do anything. These individuals will soon find that regardless of how well they have done in the past, there will be new things to learn and skills to master that will cause them great difficulty. But a confident attitude will help them stick to the challenge until they can begin to find some success, and then they will be on their way to more success.

Resiliency is a cycle just as failure is a cycle. We learn the most from experience, and when our experience is positive and successful in one or more respects, we have more of an incentive to repeat the experience. This is a positive cycle. The reverse is also true. When we try something new, for example asking a girl to a party in junior high, and she declines in a less than sensitive manner (something like, "You must be joking!"), we will remember this experience when faced with a similar challenge the next time. People don't generally like to fail or to experience rejection and ridicule. In fact, most of us will go well out of our way to avoid situations where these are possibilities. However, the world can be a tough place, and unless we can take a little ridicule, we are likely to give up before we really find out our capabilities. This process points out the need for children to learn resiliency skills as early as possible to develop an inner working model of competence along with inner confidence.

ॐॐ

Resiliency was one thing Uri possessed

Born in Russia to a mother who was a prostitute for alcohol, and drugs when she could get them, Uri was eight when I met him. Already he was the veteran of five years in a Russian orphanage, a failed adoption in the U.S., and another failed foster placement. He was considered untreatable by his psychiatrist due to his many disabilities, including: multiple sclerosis, borderline IQ, severe attachment problems, a severe speech disorder, and an angry disposition most of the time. He had trouble walking, talking, learning, and getting along with anyone, but there is one thing little Uri had and that was the ability to bounce back and keep trying. We took advantage of this one important asset. He came to our program with excitement. His positive energy quickly changed when he learned there were rules and expectations, his least favorite things. But over the next three years in three of our programs he never gave up; he learned a little more each day and gradually began to improve. There were setbacks, but an overall unmistakable positive trend. He graduated

*and moved to a family. With the right support he did
better in school, improved his speech and most of all
began to like people, whom he had never learned to
trust. Even when families and professionals had thrown
in the towel with this young boy, he never gave up.
Today he is doing very well, and with each passing year
his disabilities move closer to abilities due to one thing
he did learn in the Russian orphanage – survival meant
you can never give up, you must keep trying.*

৵৵

Our early years set the stage for much that will follow.
This begins in our brain when we adapt to the world we
find all around us. We develop neurological associations
with situations in life, with people we experience, and with
challenges we face. When we come out on top, we grow in
the confidence that we can handle the pressures and even
failures and disappointments in life. When we do not, we
learn to defend and to avoid taking risks. Beginning
surprisingly early in life, most of these experiences will
form the foundation of the way we view our self, other
people in our life, and the world around us.

Developing attachments in life is a component of the
early formation of a lifelong disposition. Since social success
and social support are essential requirements for a good
life, our ability to bond and attach with others may be the
most important early experience we have in life. But
consider when our most important attachment experiences
happen: at birth and in the hours, days and weeks
afterward. In fact, the process of bonding even begins
before birth. There may be no better example of the need for
early skill development in life than bonding and
attachment. An attachment disorder is fundamentally a
resiliency problem. When serious negative experiences take

place very early in life, our brain steps in to adapt to the situation and begins to avoid seeking support, caring and connection with others. Said somewhat differently, our brain determines that being vulnerable to others, and particularly a care provider, is just too great a risk and we stop coming back for more. Instead of sticking to the challenge of getting close to others, the child develops a disposition of giving up on relationships by avoiding them.

Whether it is attachment, confidence, or a host of other essential early developmental milestones, the early chapters of all of our life stories are some of the most important, and they set the stage for much of what will play out over the rest of our lives.

Resiliency and Trauma

Nowhere is the ability to bounce back from adversity more important than when the most difficult things happen to us and we find our ability to cope compromised. Thus trauma and resiliency are problem and solution, and need to go together if the individual is going to come out of the difficult situation in one piece in terms of mind, body, and spirit.

However, too often trauma is not followed by resiliency. Our society has all the signs of this with the many children, teens and adults who begin a cycle of failure after being traumatized. While it is usually unfair to say that victims of trauma are at fault for their post-traumatic decisions, society quickly forgets why people act in problematic or antisocial ways and focuses solely on individual responsibility and punishment. Thus, we have the largest percentage of incarcerated people of any country in the world, and we have a "war on drugs" that in part is focused on catching individuals who have turned to drugs to cope with the aftermath of trauma in their lives.

When trauma is followed by resiliency, it is possible that the traumatized individual can emerge more skilled and confident than before the traumatic event. Most of us would not choose to be traumatized, just as most of us would prefer to skip the hard lessons in life that we all receive. When an unpleasant experience presents itself, our two choices are to handle the situation or have the situation handle us. When we do the former, we develop an internal confidence and literally have our brains develop a pathway to coping.

Resiliency is best learned young and with mild to moderately difficult experiences. Watching a toddler learn to handle not getting his or her way is a study in coping. Some toddlers adjust to being disappointed and hearing "no" from a parent. Others have a meltdown that appears to be the end of life as we know it from the perspective of the child. Some children have parents who struggle with saying no, and they do not get the opportunity to develop flexibility when they do not get what they want. A child's temperament is also a factor in the way he or she responds to challenging events. Temperament is influenced by early experiences, but there is also the factor of individual differences. Like snowflakes, no two individuals are alike even when they have similar backgrounds. However, regardless of temperament, resiliency must be learned, and the sooner in life, the better for the individual.

In our treatment program we have had children come to us who have extreme reactions to not getting their way. This is more often due to traumatic experiences rather than to having been coddled. But regardless, some adults have suggested that we avoid telling the child "no" unless we want to spend the next one to two hours dealing with an emotional and behavioral meltdown. I have always viewed this differently. Our program gives such a child continual opportunities to hear "no," to not get exactly what he or she wants, and to help him or her through these experiences. In my view, it has always seemed unfair to children to have them believe that life will give them what they want. I want every child to be able to bounce back when things do not go the way the child wishes, or when things go badly for whatever reason. The only way any of us learn resiliency after disappointment is through practice.

We know from research that will be discussed in Chapter 10 that social support helps people handle stress in their lives and to become more resilient. With children, young people, and even young adults, the bad things that happen to all of us are more easily faced with the support of others. Most people face the experience of being rejected by a love interest. This usually happens in our youth and is a time that the individual needs the support of an adult. With early rejections it feels as though life is over and love will always be out of the suffering teen's grasp. We read Shakespeare's *Romeo and Juliet*, the classic love tragedy, and through the beauty of the prose it is not difficult to see the author's reflection of romantic love as a form of losing one's mind. The marriage counselor in me wonders if Romeo and Juliet had a bit more time together, would they have discovered they had little in common other than trying to get to each other? What both needed was the support of a wise individual to help them with their situation, but the good nurse and the friar dropped the ball badly in the story.

When we go through the bad times in life we need to find support, objectivity and someone with enough distance from our situation to help us see our options. When those around us run into bad times, they need us to be the wiser, more objective person who can support them in their pain and inform their higher reasoning centers. No trauma that we survive is beyond our ability to rebound from. But to do so requires resiliency skills, support, and some other ideas that will come in the following chapters.

THE PATH TO RESILIENCY

Resiliency is rebounding from adversity.

Resiliency requires that we exercise control over our own brain.

Use conscious thoughts to overcome unconscious thoughts.

Learn to turn off your brain's alarm response to non-threatening events.

Teach your brain to be calm under stress and the result will be a cycle of resiliency.

Consider your power to decide if things in your life are good or bad.

Resiliency is first learned by the example of others and then by personal experience.

Resiliency is a weave of self-confidence, experience of past success, social support, and a positive outlook.

Six

Optimism

There are many ways that a person can affect his or her life for the better, but the fostering of optimism is unsurpassed in what it brings to the individual. Optimism is an orientation and an outlook on life. The word has its roots in the Latin word "optimus," meaning best or perfection. A working definition of optimism is "A disposition or tendency to look on the more favorable side of events or conditions and to expect a favorable outcome... as well as a belief that good ultimately predominates over evil in the world" (Webster, 2001). Synonyms for optimism include confidence and hopefulness. The opposite of optimism is pessimism or being cynical in one's outlook.

Having an optimistic disposition has ripple effects throughout an individual's body, mind and spirit. Orientations to life are heavily influenced by environment, such as what a child learns growing up, or the atmosphere of the work place. I have noticed that optimism appears to go in and out of style in our culture. As technology has become more pervasive in our everyday lives, our information age provides us with instant access to what is going on in the world. It appears that having a belief that good ultimately predominates over evil in the world has been a difficult belief to maintain over time.

Optimism has been viewed for some time as somehow old-fashioned and naive. If we looked at optimism being associated with a specific time in our nation's recent history, it would be much more closely associated with the attitudes of the 1950s than before or after this decade. The 50s were a time after a great world war where our country prevailed in the struggle of good over evil, and the exploding possibilities of technology held the promise of a future of leisure and convenience. A close look at this time in our history reflects just as many challenges as any other decade. There was the Cold War, we were behind in the race for space, and there was growing danger of nuclear destruction. However, undaunted by these and other serious problems in the world and in our country, the mood was optimistic. Our societal tendency was to look at the positive side of the equation, after all, things were a great deal better than during the war years. Not only was the great world war over, but we won! The 1950s are a good example of what optimism is in that a positive disposition does not require that everything, or even most things, are going well, it just requires that we put more focus on the positive side rather than the negative side of our situation.

The 1960s, 70s, 80s and 90s were all decades that brought new twists to our collective disposition toward life and our view of the world, but over these decades there has been a growing tendency toward cynicism rather than hopefulness. There are many possible reasons for this including the war in Vietnam, a president resigning in disgrace, and a rejection of the traditional values and beliefs of the 50s. In the 1950s we seemed to collectively choose to focus more on the positive and hopeful, regardless of the conditions all around us. As living conditions continued to significantly improve over the last fifty years, our hopefulness as a nation does not appear to have kept pace. This was previously discussed in Chapter 4 and also in the book *The Progress Paradox* (Easterbrook, 2003). Another aspect of our national disposition has been a growing cynicism and a rejection of blind hope and faith to a more 'realistic' perspective that actually comes down much more on the cynical rather than hopeful side. For some time in our national disposition, to be cynical of politics, technology, religion, all societal institutions, and life itself has been in vogue or viewed as a more sophisticated outlook. This view is a rejection of an old-fashioned optimism (read naivete) of times past. A poignant example of this was my being contacted a couple years ago by a service organization that wanted to make a donation to my agency. The reason for the donation was that they were dissolving the group's remaining monetary assets because it was disbanding due to poor attendance and lack of interest. What was the service organization? The local Optimist Club!

Despite the passing of the local Optimist Club, there appears to be a resurgence of energy in optimism in many areas of our society. There is growing recognition that the power of positive thinking is not so old-fashioned after all. Dare I say it, it is almost cool again, rather than old-fashioned, to be an optimist. From medicine and psychology to political science and even economics, optimism is in once again, and this trend is not a minute too soon.

With any new societal focus such as optimism and positive psychology, there are the inevitable offshoots that can go down alternative and questionable directions. Take the recent best selling book phenomenon called *The Secret* (Byrne, 2007). The secret referred to in the title turns out to be something called the "law of attraction." This "law" is that whatever we think of we draw toward ourselves. This may sound very similar to many other related concepts such as affirmations. However, in this case positive thought comes very close to turning optimism into messianic salvation, or perhaps something close to magic. This self-help book, written by a motion picture producer, makes a pledge to its readers that the secret is similar to the genie in the magic lamp, where your every wish is granted. As a psychologist who has helped traumatized people for four decades, I hope people see through the marketing of this repackaging of the power of thinking positively. The "secret" of this book is no different than the long-held belief that optimism really works. But it does not work the same as magic, nor does it grant your every wish. We need to live a life filled with optimism and not rely on magical thinking to address very difficult challenges in life or bring us our every wish or desire.

The problem with any "get rich (or happy) quickly" scheme is that the participant may not find immediate success and the strategies do not make all one's dreams come true. One who believes the hype and does not get just what he wants may give up quickly and toss out the gold nugget along with the gravel. Optimism involves positive thinking, but this is only the beginning to living an optimistic and abundant life.

The intense criticism of *The Secret* may be somewhat unfair. The power of optimism is indeed impressive. However, it is not the optimism in the person that is as powerful as the person with optimism. This is a subtle but important distinction. A non-optimistic person cannot throw a positive thought toward a new car like rubbing the magic bottle. The outgrowth of a change in a person's overall orientation to positive thinking in life is what makes the difference, not the thought itself. This book is not the first time an actor, producer, or someone in the entertainment industry has overstated or somewhat missed the mark on an important aspect of living a full and contented life. But don't expect optimism to bring you what you want in life; you must take an optimistic approach and get what you want for yourself.

Regardless of the time in history, there have always been optimistic people for whom a positive disposition never went out of style in the same way as there have always been those who focus on what they don't have rather than what they do have. Although we are all influenced by the forces and attitudes in our environment, we have the personal ability to make this choice for ourselves if we exercise our personal power to do so. The expression, "think globally and act locally" begins with each of us. We may not be able to influence our culture for the positive or negative, but we can influence our own world, and this is the task of every person, particularly those who have experienced trauma in their lives. There is wisdom in the statement, "Change yourself and you change the world."

An Attitude—A Lifestyle

Being optimistic is fundamentally about a disposition toward ourselves, our lives, and the world around us. An optimistic person has an inner working model of hope and faith in the present and the future, regardless of the past. Going back to the Latin root of optimism meaning "best," a person who has a positive and optimistic disposition has the best chance at personal contentment in life. Whether we have to buck the trend in our family, our workplace, or society, it is unquestionably in our best interest to cultivate a positive outlook to the greatest degree that we are able. To find personal contentment, we must solidify the attitude of optimism into a lifestyle of optimism. Although this is true for everyone, nowhere is it more important than for the person who has experienced significant trauma in his or her life.

འ⊱

An optimistic orientation for life

I cannot hear the word optimism without thinking of my wife, Joyce. If you can be optimistic to a fault, she is close. However, I don't think it is a fault and most people would love to see so much of what is right with the world as she does. However, as enviable as this positive outlook is, at times it can produce challenges in our relationship. She sees what is right with nearly every situation, at times to my amazement. We will have a frustrating flat tire and she will say something like, "This is a lucky break!" I inquire at this enthusiasm for a flat tire, "And why is this lucky?" She explains, "Because we were not coming down a mountain in the rain when it happened." And she means it! Well, a month ago she set a new standard of seeing the bright side of any situation. We were driving home from dinner in the dark and she saw something in the road and said, "Did I just see a beautiful bouquet of flowers in the road back there?" I replied, "No dear, that was a cat that had been run over in the street." I am not making this up.

❧

A lifestyle is much more than an attitude. It is a very good idea to work on developing a positive attitude in situations we encounter in life, but it is much more important that we develop a positive lifestyle. A lifestyle includes habits, decisions, values, hobbies and beliefs as well as attitudes. The path to an optimistic lifestyle is the path to personal contentment.

You Can't Fool Mother Nature, or Your Body

Some years back there was a commercial for a margarine that was advertised to be so close to butter that even Mother Nature was fooled. The point was that mother nature is just not fooled very often. In the same way, we cannot fool our mind and body—either we are fundamentally optimistic or fundamentally pessimistic. There have been movements over the years that stressed positive affirmations. People would get together in large convention halls to learn how to think and act in ways consistent with positive affirmations. These movements were often linked with a goal, selling more real estate or accumulating wealth. Everyone was encouraged to shoot for the stars and see in their mind's eye their desired goal coming their direction.

Given the theme of this book it may sound inconsistent of me, but I have never liked how positive affirmations have been defined, or the movements that market the idea of using them to get what you desire. Not that there is anything wrong with either being positive or affirming our hopes and dreams. My difficulty is that too many people, who could be called "joiners," get on the bandwagon and miss the point entirely. To attend a training session and learn to see a red Cadillac with your name on it being made in Detroit, to me misplaces the focus on the final outcome rather than the step-by-step journey that will get you to your desired outcome. Personally, I have never been a big fan of affirmations that relate to wealth, power and influence. It seems to me that these can be an outgrowth of a self- actualized person, but when these are the main goal it somehow seems to miss the point. For example, if a scientist designs her career around winning a Nobel Prize, it seems to me she has mistaken a goal, a significant advancement in a professional field, with recognition. From an economic standpoint, my value is to have positive affirmations of personal growth and advancement. But there are limited resources in the universe, such as red Cadillacs, and not everyone can be a top real estate mogul or multi-millionaire.

My primary point concerning pretending to be optimistic rather than *being* optimistic is that you can't fool mother nature or your own body. Saying over and over to yourself, "I am lovable and capable" or "I will be the sales leader in my company this month," will mean very little if these are just habitual or hollow words in your mind rather than real beliefs. There is a psychological component often referred to as 'self talk' where we eventually begin to believe what we tell ourself. However, most of the time we have an inner awareness of what is going on and our mind can tell the difference between an unrealistic dream and a step in the direction of personal growth that has the chance of being realized. I present throughout this book that we can have significant influence over what our mind believes, but we must convince ourselves rather than rely on any self delusion or trickery.

There is a reason why most smokers quit their habit over and over again only to remain a smoker. There are similar reasons why over 90% of people who diet experience weight loss, then gain, lose and gain again, making weight loss a lifestyle in itself. There are chemical and even neurological explanations of nicotine addiction, and there are both physical and psychological components to weight gain and loss that are quite complex. However, the most significant battle that any addict wages is the battle within his or her mind. There are people who put down a cigarette for the last time and never smoke again, but this is not a large club when compared to all smokers. What an individual must do to change an addiction or an unwanted habit is to harness the internal power of the mind one step and one thought at a time. This is why the most widely effective addiction treatment stresses "one day at a time."

You can tell yourself anything, but your mind is not about to believe all you say. Like convincing a parent, a teacher or a partner of something, you must do and live it, and not just say it. You must build on small steps to make larger steps possible, and you must first experience limited achievable successes before you can convince your mind that your potential successes are limitless.

Which Internal Voice Wins?

We all have internal conflicts. The old expression "on the horns of a dilemma" or the newer expression "between a rock and a hard place," although somewhat different, both express external conflicts. In social psychology there is the principle called the "approach/avoidance" conflict where there is something that says "yes" and something else, perhaps equal in significance, that says "no." Periodically you will hear the term schizophrenia used to mean a split personality, someone who switches from one emotion, one behavior or even one personality to another. This is not what schizophrenia fundamentally is, but in everyday language people understand that this word helps express competing internal urges or even voices. Internal conflicts are normal and not a sign of a serious mental illness.

Internal conflicts are not just associated with schizophrenia, they are also associated with Dissociative Identity Disorder, or what formerly was called Multiple Personality. Yet another example of an internal conflict is Bipolar Disorder. Although both of these diagnoses are often misunderstood by the public, there is definitely an aspect of internal conflict in both. In everyday language people often say that internal conflicts make them feel "crazy," or they say something like, "I feel like I am losing it." The "it" in that statement infers that the person is losing touch with reality or internal stability. Internal conflicts can become extreme and even dysfunctional, as in the case of several mental health disorders. However, we all have these internal conflicts, and it is critical that we realize this to understand such internal battles.

To feel conflicted or have competing internal pulls does not mean that we are mentally ill; to the contrary this means we are mentally healthy. For example, some people who do not have such internal conflicts could be said to have a serious problem. There are people who do not struggle with a developed internal conscience. When they want something they take it regardless of the consequences. Our prisons are full of people who seriously violate the rights of others because they act solely on what they desire, rather than what is right or just. We all have healthy internal conflicts over right and wrong, over what is ours and what belongs to others, be it property, credit for a success at the office, or decision-making authority.

As a child I remember watching Walt Disney's *Wonderful World of Color*. One of the cartoons that was clearly meant to be educational was of the character Goofy who was shown in a number of situations bringing out internal conflicts. This was effectively depicted by Goofy looking over to his left shoulder and finding a miniature Goofy dressed in a bright red devil suit voicing his dark side and egocentric desires. He would then turn to his right shoulder to find a miniature Goofy dressed in white angel attire with the celestial voice of his higher self encouraging him to do the right thing. It has been many decades since I saw the cartoon, but as I remember, Goofy tried both approaches in various situations and the lesson to us kids was to resolve the internal conflict by doing the right thing. I believe in the cartoon that birds, raccoons and even a singing insect (Jiminy Cricket) would break into the song, "Always let your conscience be your guide." Devils and angels on our shoulder is a bit simplistic, but I have to hand it to Disney, his cartoon made an impression on me that I still remember many years later.

Of the many other examples of internal conflict that could be mentioned, I will add one more. Most of us have responsibilities each morning that require a schedule and the use of an alarm to start our day. It may not happen each day, but it is a common experience to go through an internal battle when the alarm goes off. This could be described as one internal voice saying, "it is just too early to get up, I'm going to lie here a bit longer." Clock manufacturers know this, and a required feature on every alarm clock is the "snooze button." However, there is another voice that says, "I don't want to be late so get out of this warm bed and into the cold world right now." This experience is so universal that we have classifications for people based on which thought prevails. We have "morning people" and we have "night people" whose internal conflict becomes how many times they allow themselves to hit the snooze button. Brain research on the right and left hemispheres is even postulating that the conflict many people have each morning could generally be described as our two brains having an argument for dominance, not entirely different than Goofy's internal conflicts.

My point is that internal conflicts are normal and healthy, within reasonable limits, and we all have them. The most fundamental voices or thoughts of internal conflicts could be boiled down to a positive or negative orientation about a specific situation or about life in general.

The negative orientation is ruled by fear, pessimism, and recalling all the times that ended badly. We all have plenty of these going back to our early years and continuing the rest of our life. We all can stop and let our memories go back in time to failures, embarrassments and small or large tragedies. Just now I remembered being nine years old and living in Nebraska across from a popcorn field. When the crop was harvested one year, the corn harvester killed a mother rabbit, leaving her eight very young baby rabbits. My brother and I found them and took them home. I cared for them, fed them and kept them warm. After several days I found one dead, and it was a terrible feeling. The next day two more were rigid and cold when I got up to feed them. Over three weeks all eight died because my best efforts were not enough of a replacement for the mother rabbit. At nine years of age this was a horrible experience of disappointment, emotional pain, and a deep sense of responsibility for the death of these wondrous furry creatures. It was not my first experience of failure, and it would not be my last.

Finding a family of wild rabbits cannot compare to the terrible negative experiences many children have of abuse and neglect, such as nights shivering under the covers while hearing their mother being beaten or waiting to see if he will come into your bed tonight and meet his sexual needs over your internal screaming objections that will not be externally expressed. Some of us were children who faced parents who let us know that we were a demanding bother, and the abortion option should have been taken in the beginning. Some of us lost parents or siblings, and most of us have lost pets that helped us face the world. Medical problems, school failures or problems, accidents, grief and loss, and many other very negative experiences form the basis of traumas that are small, medium and large. The determining factors for us all comes down to how much support we experienced and how well we were able to cope with the situation.

On the other hand, there are the wonderful times such as having a nightmare and climbing into bed with your parents and feeling the comfort that you hoped would always be there in your life, or the vacations when the whole family was discovering strange and beautiful places together. At age four I remember my first camping experience in the redwoods of California. I slept in the front seat of my uncle's pickup truck. But the strongest memory of camping was the remarkable smell of the trees and the campfire that I vividly remember today. The good times include successes, such as the last day of school in third grade with the whole wonderful summer in front of you. Positive times include maturing and having a love interest return your affection, but you can't dwell on how nearly all of them ended up. There were successes in school, with friends, with jobs, and there were good times, sunsets, moments in life when it all just made sense, or what Abraham Maslow called a "peak experience" (Maslow, 1970).

So we all have both incredibly positive experiences and phenomenally negative experiences. Now the internal conflict plays out: which voice, which thought will win out? When I face my next challenge in life, will my internal thought be that I am not able to handle this challenge — I am not smart enough or not strong enough? Or will my internal thought be that I have been through a lot and I can get through this one? In fact, I can learn from the challenge and perhaps even find some aspect of enjoyment in the process.

⤜⤛

Some of history's greatest individuals were members of the failure club

Which view do we have of experiences that happen to us? It is often easy to see how things went wrong, how situations turned out differently than we wanted. It can be easy to view our efforts as failures to reach our goal or desired result. But consider the fact that many of the most famous historical figures faced much greater failure than. we will ever experience. Abraham Lincoln lost all but one election before his easy election to the presidency. Even in his final days after the Civil War, family tragedies, and personal conflicts, he viewed himself a failure as a person. Thomas Edison invented a great many innovations, but failed continually in what he attempted. What about that electric light bulb of his? Yes, it was just another failed experiment that turned out to be lucky in his view. Michelangelo, a broken, angry man, at times not pleased with his artistic skills. Alexander the Great viewed himself as a failure because he could not manage the known world that he conquered. One of the most beloved saints was Francis of Assisi. However, on his deathbed he felt he had failed to live the right example for his followers. Clearly it is not our successes or failures in life that matter as much as our own internal judgment.

❧

We all have internal conflicts, we all have competing urges, and we all find out each morning which hemisphere of our brain will win the battle of the snooze alarm. The fundamental conflict that overshadows all of these conflicts is the positive vs. negative battleground. It is my intention to be repetitive on this issue through these chapters in saying that the internal orientation, or inner working model, that wins this battle for the positive or the negative will fundamentally determine a person's overall life experience in all aspects of life — social, personal, physical, emotional and spiritual.

It May Be Fashionable to Be a Cynic, but It Is Life-Giving to Be an Optimist

All around us we find an emphasis on the negative. Listen to a comedy routine and you will find a strong emphasis on the absurd, the contradictory, and the negative aspects of daily living. Read the news and make a mental scale of how much can be placed on the positive scale and how much on the negative scale, and watch which way the scale tips. Consider our entertainment and how many TV shows and movies are about crime, serial killers, and horror (something I have never understood the interest in); rather than uplifting, life-affirming and feel-good moments that we can add to our day. If your life is way too positive, there are many outlets that can help you bring it back into balance with strong doses of negativity.

But it is not just that our culture immerses itself in negativity—for some reason we think being cynical is smart, edgy and fashionable. We have radio talk show hosts who fill the airways with astounding nonstop verbal assaults and invectives. I don't have proof of this, but it seems the more negative a radio personality the more listeners he has. What is this about?

I read about our entertainment industry (yes, we even turn enjoyment into an industrialized complex primarily focused on making money) and wonder why it is courting failure for a movie to be "G" rated. Why does Hollywood make sure there is sufficient violence and profanity to obtain at least a "PG-13" if not an "R" rating? Is it just me, or are today's PG-13 shows more like the R rated shows of the past? The argument is often made that it is unfair to blame the producers of a product when they are simply meeting the desires of the consumer. Such an argument can be made for purveyors of alcohol, tobacco, gas-guzzling cars, pornography, assault rifles and, perhaps, the nightly TV news. I understand that the one profitable industry over time on the internet is adult pornography. This is the case because of millions of personal choices made by people each day. If more people go to a violent movie than a romantic comedy, this helps explains an industry trend, but it does not bring more positive energy into our lives and our culture.

Perhaps an important point here is that we need to change our tastes if we don't like what we are being fed. But wait, isn't a good violent movie with chase scenes just what the doctor ordered after a difficult week at work, or dealing with your teenager at home? You may think this fits for you. But as with alcohol, nicotine, sex with a stranger, caffeine, and sugar, is the short-term gratification buzz worth the long-term impact on your life?

It is not my intent to change Hollywood or even the TV evening news, which I drifted away from many years ago because I had ample problems of my own without adding the problems of the world each day. I know I will offend some of you with this example, but if people no longer wanted to see dead bodies, knives penetrating flesh and medical examiners doing autopsies in low-cut dresses, then *CSI* would no longer be on TV, much less be the top show. My intent is to ask you to look at what you fill your brain with each day and weigh this on the positive/negative scale. Like the internet, each of us chooses what sites we visit each day. In the same way we choose our movies, our meals, our company, and yes, our thoughts, our feelings and our behaviors. So my intention is to have you look at the world you are creating.

It is hard to understand why being positive is not very fashionable these days. There was a time that even on TV the top show for many years was Bill Cosby's lovable and funny father dealing with family life and usually coming up with a happy ending for the show. I have a copy of the movie *The Ten Commandments* and I still get inspired by Cecil B. Demille's corny production more than *The Passion of The Christ* (sorry, Mel). I think for me this has to do with seeking the positive in a story. I will show that I am terribly out of fashion, but I cannot watch a horror movie because my brain takes snapshots of images and puts them in my mental scrapbook. I don't watch the nightly news. I will not watch an "entertainment" show about a serial killer, and I refuse to sit through a comedian's angry rant laced with continual course language. None of this adds to my life anything that I want.

Like our diet, I think we can and need to cultivate our taste in preferences. If babies are given a choice between blended lima beans and ice cream, most will choose the latter. But we are not babies, and it is in our best interest to make continual choices toward what makes us stronger and not just choose what is "tasty." The many ways that we can build more positive components into our lives are what make us stronger. There is no limit to what this may look like in your life. It may be a healthy diet, or what you read, how you deal with others, or how you relieve stress. These are the thousands of decisions each day that can add or take away from your bank account of positivity. It seems to be fashionable to be sarcastic, cynical, and negative, but if you want to improve your life you will need to forgo whatever drains your psychological and spiritual batteries, and pursue positive charges whenever and wherever you can find them.

Positive Emotions Make a Major Difference in Living

A positive outlook is directly related to positive emotions. How we feel is directly connected to how we think and how we act. A hypothesis has been developed that positive emotions initially were critical to signal to others that there was an absence of threat in the interaction. This no doubt has some influence on why people are attracted to people who reflect positive emotions. But there are other possibilities as to why positive people have all the fun, whether they are blond or not. People with positive emotions tend to do better in all aspects of life than more negative people. They also are more productive, more socially engaged, and it would follow that they also have higher incomes (Diener, 2000; Judge, Thorese, Bono, Patton, 2001).

People who have consistent positive emotions can develop a perpetuating cycle where positive emotions lead to positive thoughts that in turn contribute to further happiness (Ryan & Deci, 2001). This goes into the dynamic that positive people perceive their world in more positive ways than those with negative orientations. Positive people better internalize their goals increasing their changes to meet them. It is no surprise that positive people are more active in social and community gatherings, both of which have been found to be associated with greater happiness in life (Halliwell & Pittman, 2004).

In addition to all the other advantages of positive affective states, Fredickson proposes that positive emotions broaden the creativity of thought, alternatives of actions and even build upon the cognitive resources of the individual. There appears to be little doubt coming from research that positive emotions directly impact cognitive processes, cognitive appraisal, and also social relationships (Fredickson, 2004). And did I mention that positive people live longer (Huppert & Whittington, 1995; Danner, Snowdon & Friesen, 2001)? Clearly, positive emotions add to the quality of life, but they do not exist in a vacuum and are directly related to our perceptions.

We Live in the World We Perceive

In politics there is an expression, "perception is reality." We can extend this statement to our lives as well. What we perceive to be our reality essentially becomes our reality. This dynamic occurs on multiple levels. What we tend to notice becomes more salient or important to us. For example, you hear from a coworker that someone in the office has been talking behind your back and not in complimentary ways. The next time you are in the same room with this person, this knowledge is going to heighten your awareness of every minor detail regarding the person, her behavior and her words. In this way what we are thinking determines our focus and our experience.

We all have a fundamental disposition toward our life and the world around us. I have called this an inner working model, an expression that comes from the attachment theory of John Bowlby, M.D. (Bowlby, 1982). Our inner working model forms our thoughts and our feelings about our world. This inner model could include an awareness of the abundance all around us, that includes wonderful people, the wonders of nature, and perhaps the grace and benevolence of God. Or your inner working model may be more built upon a view of scarcity, with a focus on the struggles of human existence, knowing that we will someday lose everything we care about and ultimately the short time we have in the vale of tears. A person who has either of these two models will likely approach every day and every task differently. We cannot help but be affected by the internal orientation of our awareness, our thinking, and our resulting emotional response to our experiences.

Our inner working model is something that is fundamental to all of us. It is something of a default mode to our life. If you expect trouble, sure enough you find it. Or if you are the proverbial child in the pile of manure saying "I know there is a pony in here somewhere," then you will find your pony in most situations. Our thoughts and feelings, and therefore our behavior, are significantly affected by our inner model. But it is also true that we can impact our inner working model with some effort. If you are tired of being a negative person, it may be difficult to change, but it is not impossible and will be worth your effort to change. Our inner working model is another way that our perceptions become reality. If you talk to chronically depressed people, they are convinced that life is a dead end road with potholes. If you talk to a chronic optimist, every hurdle in life is there to make us smarter, stronger and more confident that ever before. Which person is right? Both live in the world they perceive.

Many people have emotional problems. In our culture, we prefer to look anywhere but within to find the cause, and for that matter, the solution. There are anxious people who have too much stress in their lives. Perhaps this is true, but there are many other people who live with stress and do not have problems with anxiety. There are sad and depressed people who all have reasons to feel badly about the world they live in and believe they cannot escape from. There are angry people who see all the reasons that any reasonable person would be angry as well if the same situation had happened to them. However, most drivers come across other inconsiderate drivers without developing road rage and needing the rest of the day to calm down. The reality is that, other than emotional problems produced by imbalances of chemical receptors in the brain, feelings arise out of what we tell ourselves is going on around us. Did that jerk intentionally cut you off on the freeway? It depends on what you told yourself. Are you a nervous wreck because of your job, or are you a nervous wreck because you tell yourself your job is ruining your life?

For all of us, what we perceive is what we get. Imagine a world much like the holodeck of the Starship Enterprise in *Star Trek*. Whatever we want for a reality, the master computer creates for us. But wait, we don't need the Enterprise because we are busy every day telling the master computer, our brain, what we want to experience. If that just does not ring true for you, do yourself a favor and finish this book before dropping it into the paper recycling bin. Your brain is not the master computer, it is much more powerful in nearly all respects than any computer that has ever been produced. Your brain is the most complex organic structure in the known universe, and it is fully capable of creating the reality that you desire. If you believe that you can't alter your perceptions, your emotions and your reality, you are in a prison of your own making. Let's see if we can loosen the prison bars just a little.

Quantum Physics and Psychology

In Chapter 9 we will take a quick trip to the fascinating world of quantum physics, but you need to prepare

yourself for a bumpy ride. The hard science of physics is now showing remarkable convergence with the softer science of psychology. Be prepared to read how the study of the subatomic world of matter and energy that forms the basic foundations of our material world is pointing to physical explanations of psychological principles. For example, would you be interested in an explanation of how our positive thinking directly changes our material world? How about a scientific basis for how our thinking can affect the events in our lives?

Would it surprise you to read in a physics text, and not just in a psychology text, that if you want to change your life then you should change the way you think and the way you feel. Would you be interested in a description of how molecules and atoms work and how this helps explain everything we have discussed in this chapter? Am I implying that there is scientific evidence from the physical sciences to support all this positive psychology talk? Yes, that is exactly what we will consider a little later.

THE PATH TO OPTIMISM

Optimism is positive thinking put into action and expecting favorable outcomes.

Optimism is a lifestyle, not just a type of thinking.

Optimism is the best path to personal contentment.

False optimism is not effective. We must believe in what we are about, one situation at a time.

Will we listen to the positive voice within or the pessimistic voice? We all have both.

Take a close look at the thoughts, feelings and behaviors you choose every day.

Optimism involves thousands of daily decisions we make involving all aspects of our life.

SEVEN

PHYSICAL HEALTH - THE MIND/ BODY CONNECTION

Now more than ever before there is ample evidence that our mind and body are integrally linked. What our mind sees, our body gradually becomes. We see this in optimistic and pessimistic people. It would seem unfair if everyone didn't have the same opportunities in life to pursue their dreams, but for those who think positive, they not only have a more positive life, but they have more positive health as well. For those who look at the negative side of nearly everything, they have more physical problems and poorer health, among other self-inflicted challenges.

How does the body take positive thoughts and turn them into positive states of health? This has been noticed for hundreds of years, and we are learning more all the time about this dynamic. But there is a Nobel Prize in Medicine still out there waiting for someone who more clearly unlocks the keys to the mind/body connection.

The body is able to do a great many things that medicine acknowledges, but how the body performs in some areas remains somewhat mysterious. This is especially true for those of us who are not physiologists. For example, none of us question the ability of our body to heal a cut finger, but do any of us know just how this takes place? So much of the body is beautifully designed to promote health and survival. It almost seems as though the body can heal itself, including in mind and spirit, if we do not get in the way. Perhaps optimists have learned some internal method of capitalizing on the body's healing ability, while the pessimist gets in the way of this natural ability.

Historically there has been more interest in Eastern rather than Western approaches to self-mastery activities such as meditation, contemplation and mind over matter. As a child I saw depictions of whirling dervishes, yogis sitting on beds of nails and skinny holy men with their begging bowls all made out to be silly oddities. As Hans Selye and others began to find that mental strength was a pathway to health (Selye, 1946), the mental power of Eastern thought became more than a parlor trick, and more interesting to the pragmatic Western world.

Most of us have experienced that we have the ability to make ourselves ill. We face a tough experience that we wish to avoid and our stress begins to break down our resistance to a cold or flu. We have also had times where we were just too invested in something important to allow ourselves any chance of coming down with an illness. In those moments we seem to, at least briefly, experience that the mind/body connection can be a strong factor in our health or lack of health.

One would think that the ability to have great mental influence over one's health would be a welcome thought. However, for many people the prospect of determining one's health is just too much responsibility, and they would rather leave that up to the "bug that is going around," or get the over-the-counter medication that they can rely on to bring some health or at least pain relief. To some people, doing their part to stay healthy means to stop by the neighborhood drug store. If we can influence our health, then we can influence our illnesses. Some think that if they take all this control over their health too seriously, then they will have to take responsibility to quit smoking, stop overeating, start exercising, and not drink to excess—in other words, give up what some people view as the fun stuff in life. You will hear such a person say something like, "You have to die of something, and I'd rather die fat, happy and with a cigarette dangling from my mouth than die of worry." However, if these people spent any time in a hospital they would find that dying of emphysema, diabetes, or other illnesses directly related to lifestyle choices is anything but dying happy.

Our medication-obsessed society encourages people to sit back, do whatever they like and medicate themselves later if needed. My favorite example is the tablet that is marketed to be taken before going out and getting drunk. The concept is to use the pill to lessen the impact of our poor choices. I have another proposed product that I would call the "Smarttab." Just take this pill, then don't drink to excess and give yourself credit for being smarter than the people who waste their money on alcohol they didn't need, then say things they shouldn't say, do things they shouldn't do, and pay for all this afterwards.

Ease and Dis-ease

In a lecture on the mind/body connection many years ago, a presenter said something I was hearing for the first time. He spoke of illness as dis-ease. This statement has stuck with me ever sense. It may be one of the best ways to describe physical illness as the body being in a state of dis-ease. The human body strives for balance in all areas, we have the sympathetic nervous system or on-button and the parasympathetic nervous system or off-button. We have a balance of sodium in our blood, not too much and not too little. We have a Ph balance in the body with acidity and alkalinity. Nearly everywhere in the body there is a pull toward balance. But what happens when the many important elements of balance are not maintained? The results may be that the body either dies, begins to shut down, or goes into a state of illness or dis-ease.

I once heard a naturopath say that the common cold was a healthy step for the body to regain balance. The theory seemed to be that the body needed to change its chemistry and its status because it needed to get back in balance. This sounds like the explanation that meteorologists use to describe a large storm such as a hurricane. Hurricanes can be viewed as a way the planet releases extra energy to return to more balance in the atmosphere. But does the body have a similar process during illness? I do not know the answer, but I suspect not. In fact, I would say that it is quite the opposite in that illness in the body is the lack of balance and not an attempt to regain balance. It may be that some of the body's methods to address illness could be thought of as symptoms of the illness, when in fact they are part of the body's healing process. For example, if you are unfortunate enough to pick some poison ivy or poison oak with a bouquet of wild flowers, the red itchy skin is not the illness but the body's attempt to fight off the invading chemical irritant. What is clear is that the body cannot maintain a state of serious imbalance or dis-ease for long periods of time without serious consequences.

The need for balance in the body puts the pressure on its healing capacity to assist with striving for equilibrium. Although the body does a great many things without the assistance of the conscious mind, we are growing in our understanding of the many ways the mind can help. Biofeedback is one method where the active involvement of the mind can have a major influence over systems in the body that in the past were categorized as "involuntary." For example, with just a little practice, most people can be taught to influence their skin temperature. Most of us would not know where the skin thermostat is to be able to raise or lower the temperature of our hands or feet. But this turns out to be rather easily learned. In a similar way, voluntary control can influence brain waves, heart rate, muscular tension, blood pressure, stress levels, and even our immune system. How the body does all this is not yet completely clear, but there is little question at our current understanding of medical science that we have considerably more voluntarily influence over "involuntary systems" in the body than once believed.

It is now common to find patients being asked to actively assist in their healing with many medical conditions. I am talking about much more than diabetics making sure they get their insulin, and patients with emphysema not smoking. Considering the profound influence of something as straightforward as optimism or positive thinking, medical professionals would be missing a major ingredient in healing to overlook the mental state of the patient. We now find those going into surgery encouraged to think positively. This is more than being hopeful, it appears clear from research that this form of active thought can align the body's own healing capacities to join with the medical procedure. This can include surgery, radiation and chemotherapy, anesthesia, and the effectiveness of medication in general.

৯৬

Mind over anesthesia

I once conducted my own experiment with using my mind to influence an anesthetic. I was twenty-seven, with ten years of meditation training, and also doing biofeedback training as well. I had to have oral surgery to extract wisdom teeth that were in my jaw sideways. The oral surgery was more complex than usual and they would extract all four at the same time. I asked permission to test the influence of my mental ability to affect the anesthesia. The anesthesiologist smiled and said he had no problem with my experiment. I interpreted the smile as a belief that my mind was no match for his chemical cocktail. As he gave me the anesthesia in my arm, I felt immediately euphoric and I focused my mind on the awareness of the sensation. After five minutes, he noticed I was not in slumberland. He gave me a second shot. I became groggy but stayed focused. Ten minutes later the oral surgeon was impatient to begin. It was a challenge but I was able to speak, to move my arms and legs, and I felt like I was hanging onto a rope to maintain consciousness. The surgeon said the experiment had to stop, I received a third dose and I mentally let go of the rope and was out immediately. With much more anesthesia than normal, they had a difficult time bringing me back, which resulted in getting pain medication late, and I had 30 minutes without pain medication, an experience I remember well. I have always remembered this experiment in the power of my mind over outside influences.

ॐॐॐ

We saw in the first chapter that the stress response cycle can adversely affect our emotional and physical health. When we poorly handle stressors that are both large and small, the body keeps score. If the stress in our lives overwhelms us, we define the problem as more than we can cope with. When this happens in the mind, there are concurrent impacts on the hormonal or chemical balance of the body. The release of excessive reactive hormones can result in a habitual cycle that over time breaks down the body and brings dis-ease to the delicate balance.

We found in chapter 5 that with the influence of the conscious mind, the stress response cycle cannot only be influenced, but the resulting impact can be reversed. It is not stress in our lives that causes physical problems, but our internal perception and response to the stress that makes the difference. Perception, response, and extrinsic memory are all important components of the mind. When we bring the power of our conscious mind to bear on a problem in our life, the mind/body connection can be utilized to enhance health or achieve other desirable goals.

ॐॐ

William had skills of which he was unaware

William had a very difficult life during his first seven years. He had most everything going against him. He had been the victim of serious neglect and physical as well as sexual abuse. He had serious problems with self-regulation and was diagnosed as hyperactive. He had learning disabilities and was frequently violent and could not handle any level of stress without tantrums that could be measured on the Richter Scale. In short, it was a real challenge to know where we could begin to help this child when he came into our program. Few interventions had any positive impact on his many issues. Almost in desperation, at one point I decided to teach William to relax and introduced him to meditation. He liked new things and agreed to work with me. We relaxed together (marginally effective), we then did some visualization (more effective), and then I asked him to join me in a day at the beach. William sat relaxed and was encouraged to close his eyes and see himself sitting in the warm sun on a tropical beach by some palm trees. I watched as he noticeably relaxed his tense and hyperactive body movements. We were both quiet for a while until William finally whispered, "Dave, I'm getting hot in the sun, can I move under the palm tree?" To my surprise I had found a way through William's mind to impact his body, and we capitalized on this as his treatment continued.

ॐॐ

The Evidence that We Create Our Own Health or Illness

I have made a number of claims about the ability of the mind to influence the body. It is time to provide some scientific evidence of these claims. The following are just a few of hundreds of examples of research reflecting the influence of the mind/body connection either contributing to or damaging the health of the individual.

- *Hopefulness and curiosity protected against hypertension, diabetes and upper respiratory infection* (Kubzansky & Kawachi, 2001). Yes, you read that right, the patient's attitude made a significant different in how major illness affected the cardiovascular, endocrine and respiratory systems of the body.
- *Men with a positive outlook had one half the rate of heart disease, cardiovascular disease, chronic obstructive pulmonary disease, colds and premature death.* If you could come up with a pill that would do all this, it would outsell even Viagra! But you don't even need to spend money on a pill, just have a more positive outlook.
- *Patients who reported being content with their lives had a 50% increase in the response of antibodies to flu vaccine* (Davidson, 2004). How could feeling good about your life affect the way a vaccine works? The answer is

under investigation by researchers, but in the meantime being content sounds like just what the doctor ordered.

- *Positive emotions assist cardiovascular functioning* (Middleton & Byrd, 1996). Since more people in the United States die every year of heart problems than all other causes of death combined, some positive emotions couldn't hurt, and they just might help — a lot!
- *Being positive improves recovery from surgery* (Carver & Scheier, 2005). The main point here comes back to being positive. The other point may be to recover a while before you look at the bill for the surgery!
- *Positive people have fewer heart attacks* (Kubzansky, Sparow, Vokonas & Kawachi, 2001). When it results in fewer heart problems, what is the down side of being positive? I guess you just might run the risk of feeling too good about your life.
- *Positive people have fewer medical problems and heal more quickly* (Aspinwall & Leaf, 2002). So we can expand the benefits of being positive to protecting us from all types of physical problems. But the benefits don't stop there: if we do get sick, we get better faster.
- *Positive people live longer* (Danner, Snowden & Friesen, 2001). Enough with all this positive talk, so what if being positive helps your heart, your recovery from surgery and protects you from medical problems and helps you heal faster. All this means you would just have to live longer, and that is exactly what these researchers found.

Exercise—The Medicine Few People Take

This will not be the first time you have heard the following — the majority of Americans are overweight at all ages, and the trend line has been going up each year for the last forty years. This is a commonly quoted fact in the media, but the reality is that this news has not changed our habits.

At the same time, between 1/3 and 1/2 of Americans lead sedentary lives (depending upon the age group). There has never been a question in the medical and psychology world that activity and exercise can have profound influences on the body, mind and spirit. In fact it may be the best medicine for health that we have available to us, but few people seem interested in this wonder "drug."

As medical science gets more sophisticated, we are able to pinpoint more precisely what activity and exercise do for the human body. Throughout history the amount of activity a person was involved in was not a meaningful discussion. People were active because they had to be. They hunted, they gathered, they worked the farms and fields, they did hard physical labor, and without the modern conveniences of machines that did the work for them, they had to do a great amount of physical work every day. In the past, it was only the lords and ladies that had the choice of how much activity they involved themselves in. Now the average American has more conveniences than the super-wealthy of past generations. We no longer have to be very active in life, and the results are showing. The promise fifty years ago that technology would make our lives better by reducing how much work we had to do has been realized, but has it made our lives better?

The two factors that combine to produce the current state of physical health in America are the abundance of food (requiring daily restraint) and the lack of physical activity needed to survive (requiring decisions to be active). The result is the least active we have been in our nation's history.

There is an antidote for this problem, and it is exercise. Exercise has been found to decrease weight without an expensive weight loss program. It has been shown to prevent cancer, osteoporosis, heart disease, diabetes and high blood pressure, along with a host of other health advantages. While exercise prevents bad things from happening, it also does very good things such as improving mood (at least after you are done exercising), helping cope with stress, and prolonging your life. But these facts are already well known, and yet as a society we continue our slide toward less activity.

Although there are many advantages of exercise that most of us have heard about, there is a growing amount of information about the advantages of exercise on our brain. Among the many new findings of how exercise assists the brain are the following:

- Exercise promotes the development of new nerve cells or neurogenesis.
- Exercise promotes better brain functioning and increases intelligence.
- It also promotes the proliferation of synaptic connections among neurons in the brain.
- Exercise promotes learning and using the mental skills that we possess by enhancements such as bringing more blood to the brain.
- Exercise strengthens neurons to aid in their functioning.
- Exercise affects the size and strength of brain cells as much as it does muscular cells. (Ratey, 2007)

The above is not an exhaustive list of the advantages of exercise on the functioning of the brain, but it would seem to be enough when combined with the physical and emotional advantages to encourage active lifestyles and vigorous exercise on a scale we have not seen before. But the opposite is true. Other people not listening to the discovery of this real fountain of youth should not discourage you from paying attention and then doing something about bringing all these benefits into your life. It is definitely the smart thing to do to promote your own health.

Can We Laugh Our Way to Health?

The evidence appears strong that we can use our mind/body connection to positively influence our health. But how far can we take this; can simple steps like having more fun and laughing more influence our health? The answer appears to be a resounding yes.

Thirty years ago a business executive named Norman Cousins was diagnosed with cancer. Not an individual to give up on any challenge, he publicly announced that he would cure himself of the cancer by his own unorthodox methods (Cousins, 1979). For the next few years, he increased the amount of positive enjoyment he found in his life and specifically made sure that he laughed long and hard every day. He told of reading funny stories, watching funny movies, including *The Three Stooges*. Not someone to go half-heartedly into anything, he was not content to smile throughout the day. He made sure he had frequent belly laughs, and he approached humor as he had approached business, full speed ahead. He was something of a media darling with this story and I am sure that most observers skeptically waited for the cancer to prevail in the end. Over time Cousins turned the tide on his battle with a terminal physical disease that before this time was viewed as immune from our mental influence, much less being influenced by laughter. As you might already know, Norman Cousins prevailed over his cancer and began his second career lecturing and sharing with others the control over our bodies that we hold in our minds.

Many years later we have more than anecdotal evidence of humor influencing our health. There is growing medical evidence of this connection between humor and health. Here are just three of many examples of research findings in this area:

- Laughter reduces stress hormones and is associated with lower blood pressure and a lower risk of heart

attacks and arrhythmia (Berk, Felten, Tan, Bittman, & Westengard, 2001).
- Laughter increases positive feelings (Bachorowski & Owren, 2001).
- Laughter strengthens the immune system (Mahoney, Burroughs & Lippman, 2001).

If we can laugh our way to health, then we must be able to have a significant impact on our health in a variety of other ways as well. This appears to have scientific support. Now that we know we can influence our health, is the reverse just as true that we can directly influence our illness? There is little question that this is also true. Risky behaviors such as intravenous drug use, smoking, excessive alcohol consumption, and unprotected sex with strangers can all have very negative influences on the body, and each is a conscious decision we make. These may seem extreme examples to some people, although the total number of people who engage in one or more of the above behaviors is nearly one out of every three adults in the United States. On a less extreme level, what about the influence we can have on our health with not enough exercise (now we are talking about 80% of Americans), too much sugar and soft drinks in our diet or a poor diet in general? Let's consider whether it makes sense that if we can positively impact our health, then we have to take responsibility for our illness.

Are We Responsible for Our Illness?

In our blaming culture, we find ways to turn the best of fortune into a problem. The fact that we have much more influence over our ability to heal ourselves has quickly turned into a blaming question of, "If we can heal ourselves, then are we responsible for making ourselves ill?" Although this is a negative twist on a positive situation, it bears some response.

There are many things that can make us ill: harmful bacteria, viruses, accidents, stress, and a host of other causes. Few of these do we have complete control over, but with most we can have some influence. The Surgeon General tells us that washing our hands may be the most effective prevention for illnesses. Washing our hands is simplistic, but is also symbolic of keeping our body clean from harmful germs and from risky behavior.

ॐॐ

The price was just too high for this type of togetherness

A number of years ago I was the family therapist for a family that was very cohesive. They worked, played and did most everything together, so they had no problem when I told them I wanted the whole family involved with the therapy. Communication was somewhat of a challenge because the father had lost nearly all his hearing. I noticed that all the rest of the family was showing signs of significant hearing loss. When I asked about this I was told that they were aware of the hearing loss and knew the cause. It turned out that the family was made up of champion speed water skiers. Most of the family members had gone more than 100 miles an hour on water skis. To do this they had to stand directly behind massive engines with sound decibels close to jet engines. The father told me that hearing problems were simply a price they had to pay. I was appalled at this trade off, skiing fast vs. losing your hearing. What I found unacceptable and intentionally damaging, they chose to live with. However, an adult may make such a decision for him or herself, but in my view has no right to choose this for a child, as in the case if this family. I have often wondered, but I do not

*know if I influenced this family from making this
decision to act in a way that was robbing the whole
family of the wonderful sense of hearing.*

∂∾ॐ

Although we may have some culpability, for many of
the illnesses we come across in life, it is of little value for us
to blame ourselves, and blame and shame do little to bring
about health. Few of us go out of our way to become ill.
Perhaps we put in long hours at work and allow our career
stress to wear down our immune system. Perhaps we eat
poorly or do not allow our body the sleep we really need to
face a new day with the energy we need. When we realize
our internal ability to heal, we can make the changes
necessary to produce a more positive outcome. It is of little
value to self-blame rather than to self-correct.

There are some exceptions to letting ourselves off the
hook of personal responsibility. When we make consistent
decisions that we know will result in significant harm to our
bodies, our minds or our spirits, there is no avoiding
responsibility for making ourselves ill. Some of these
situations are clear and familiar: smoking, risky sex, drug
abuse, non-compliance with medical instructions, and other
such decisions. Some of these situations are somewhat less
obvious, but no less impactful. When we push our support
system away for no good reason (and there are no good
reasons to push away our support system), we will pay the
price of our self-harming decision. If we put all our energy
into our work and ignore our partner or our children, we
need to have a very direct conversation with ourself
because the results are bound to be negative for everyone.

The Mind/Body Connection for Traumatized People

The influence of the mind over the body is powerful and can work in either of two directions. We can use our minds to heal and strengthen our bodies, or we can allow the damage to our mental disposition caused by traumatic experiences to diminish and bring dis-ease to our physical self as well as our emotional and spiritual selves. The good news is that if either is possible, there is hope that we can use our mind/body connection to facilitate health if we only learn how to do this.

The *how* comes down to some form of thinking, feeling and acting in more positive ways. This just seems too easy and simplistic for some people, and they look for complex answers. An example of looking for the complex rather than simple answer can be seen in losing weight. It is just too simple to take in fewer calories and/or burn off more calories than you take in. Many look for complicated formulas, exotic menus and a world that revolves around eating. When people do this they nearly guarantee that they will not be able to maintain the solution, and failure usually is the result.

Having our mind bring health to our body requires a fundamentally negative person to change this orientation. It requires a person with fear, anxiety, anger and sadness to become someone who enjoys and who looks at the bright side of situations he finds himself in. Although such a person may periodically pay a visit to frustration and anger land, he does not stick around and live there.

We live in an instant culture that promotes looking outside of ourselves too often for the answer. This frequently means that we look to a quick external cure for our negativity, such as medicine. The pharmaceutical companies don't mind this at all. I want to be clear that I am not speaking against medication for depression or anxiety problems. However, I am saying that medication is only one way to address the problem of negative moods or states of mind. In the same way that I give children medication and tell them that this will help, but they must do their part in internally managing thoughts, feelings or behaviors, I would give a traumatized adult the same message. When every possibility is considered as a route to health, happiness and personal contentment, there are many preferred routes other than a trip to the drug (or liquor) store.

If we don't look for complex solutions for straight-forward issues, we are left with the challenge of facing a difficult world with a more positive disposition and inner working model. The challenge for traumatized people is that their view of self, others and the world has been radically impacted by trauma. When we have been neglected we see scarcity in the world. When we have a disability due to a trauma, we see all the people with abilities we don't have all around us. But the start of a more positive world begins in the brain—we have to change our thinking, one thought at a time.

There are many approaches available in any self-help section of the bookstore to help you change your thinking. There are approaches that have been around for thousands of years, such as meditation. There are intellectual approaches that help you think your way to being more positive, such as Norman Vincent Peale's *Power of Positive Thinking* (Peale, 1946). There are psychological methods such as cognitive behavioral therapy. These are just a few examples that indicate that we have known the benefit of being positive for a very long time, it is just that many of us are not very good at using the power of our positive thoughts.

The classic statement in therapy is that you only achieve your goals when you want to change. This is actually only the first step, but it is an important step. Do you want to be a more positive person? Why? I believe it needs to be for better reasons than to win friends and influence people, although these are certainly not bad goals.

I believe if we want to use "the secret" of positive thinking, it should be for something more than a new Lexus. I think we need the desire to be a more positive person because we love our self enough to set our sights on success, happiness and life satisfaction. Without a deep desire to reach the base camps on Mt. Everest, we will never have the force of will to climb to these lofty perches. Of course, the bind is we have to have enough confidence to make the climb in order to lift our spirits and our confidence by reaching the top. We must start by finding enough confidence to take the first step.

Perhaps that is the starting place — taking the first step. A process first step might be to do a personal inventory and identify what needs to change and who and what you would like to be. A practical step is just that — putting one foot in front of the other, or making one positive effort at a time. For a traumatized person I suggest that you get help. If you have a wise friend, or trusted person in your life, bring them along on the journey. If not, find a therapist who you can pay to help you see yourself and coach you along the path. Just like many other successes in life, being a more positive person is going to involve feeling the support from others in your life.

Becoming a more positive person can also be achieved by becoming more self-aware. I call this the internal witness. This is the part of me where I turn on my ability to observe myself while I live my life in order to watch how I am doing. This may sound a bit strange to some people that I go into a tense meeting, and the whole time I struggle in the meeting I am watching myself and how I am handling the situation. However, this is not a skill available to everyone and I have noticed that trauma actually helps train people to do this. Children who have been traumatized often develop keen awareness of what they focus on. They could be focused on safety or on what a particular person is doing. What such a person needs to do is to be able to turn this intensive focus on oneself.

You can start by taking a self-inventory, determining who you are and what you want to do (like being a more positive person). Next, have you put together a support system? Particularly for traumatized individuals, an ample support system may include professional guidance. Have you developed your internal witness to focus on yourself? Then all you have to do is get to work. Just like the fact that there are no easy or mysterious complex answers, there is really only concerted effort to bring more positive energy and health into your life.

Once you are engaged in this journey, one of the early detours along the way is your belief that you are failing at your attempts to succeed. Your witness needs to jump in here and see that this is just more of the negative thinking that you are working to move beyond. When a negative thought comes up, it is a good idea to replace it with a realistic but positive observation. For example, when I speak to someone I do not like, I think "This time I am going to at least not allow them to irritate me." Within minutes I want to strangle the person and I tell myself, "You are such a loser, you couldn't last two minutes with this bozo." Right then you could replace that thought with, "I had the right goal this time and next time I will go longer without being upset by this person." This is real, it is accurate and it gives you positive credit for a positive reason—thus you have taken a step toward being a more positive thinker, a more positive feeler and a more positive actor. We will come back to this topic later.

THE PATH TO PHYSICAL HEALTH

The body has natural ways of healing physically, emotionally and spiritually.

The first step is to make good lifestyle choices.

The body strives for balance; do your part to help rather than hurt this balance.

Thinking positively about healing can be as important as medication and a medical procedure.

Stress must be managed to maintain health.

Scientific research indicates a positive outlook is the best medicine.

Laughter and enjoyment help maintain health.

EIGHT

PERSONAL CONTENTMENT BEGINS WITH SOCIAL SUCCESS

As human beings, we cannot deny the fact that we are social creatures. Like bees, fish and most birds, we flock together. We don't get along as well as many other creatures, but we can't seem to live with, or live without each other. I work everyday with traumatized children who are discovering that they know very little about our social world. After all, peers are there so we can have someone to beat in videogames, right? These children seek out others when they need something that the other person has. I am always fascinated by how social all the children get right after the Christmas gifts are opened. It always starts the same, "Do you want to play? OK, let's play with your new toys." These children project their motivations onto others. If other people seek them out, the child knows that the other person must want something. Understanding the motives of others and growing in an understanding of how you meet someone, how you make and keep a friend, and how you let someone else know that you are attracted to them are some of the most challenging steps most of us have to take in life.

I watch other social animals and how well they seem to get along, unlike people. Look up at the power line sometime at a flock of pigeons sitting next to each other. They look like they all have a built-in measuring stick and they do not invade the space of the pigeon next to them, unlike my children. I wondered how they learn to understand this social distance. Observing them, I notice that the precise space in between each bird is exactly the distance it will take for them all to spread their wings unencumbered and take to flight if needed. Schools of fish seem to form one organism although there can be thousands of individual fish, turning in unison. Is there such a thing as an anti-social fish? It would seem that if one fish decided to be a free spirit and turned the wrong way, there would be trouble in the school for sure. Bees and ants are similar where guard bees will sting intruders when needed and in doing so end their lives without fanfare. But learning social conventions for humans is quite different than our fellow social creatures.

As social creatures, we are fascinated by the rare individuals who are hermits or recluses. We seem fascinated because we wonder how they do it. Who do they go to when they hurt, when they need some help, when they just want to be with someone. There are many more social isolates than recluses or hermits. These people live around others, but just don't interact in socially constructive ways. But even the most isolated people are not as solitary as they may appear to be.

Some years ago I traveled around and visited cloistered communities of men and women who chose to simplify their lives for spiritual reasons. This often meant that they lived alone, they lived together but did not talk to others, or they did not interact with the outside world. There is a very long tradition of the eremetical (hermit) life in spiritual communities. I remember traveling to Big Sur, California and driving way up on a bluff 1,000 feet above the Pacific Ocean to the Camaldolese hermits, a religious order with its roots in France. I was greeted by Brother Louis. He was a pleasant jovial man who seemed pleased to tell me all about the lifestyle of the hermits living on the edge of the bluff, and on the edge of society. I asked him why he was the official greeter if he also was a hermit. He looked at me and with a rather wild look in his eye he said, "Well, you see, I was alone too long and I began to believe that I was an angel, so they have me spending time with our guests, and I am better now." As disconcerting as it was to be talking to such an unusual man who was admitting having trouble knowing what was reality, it made perfect sense. For the hermits of Big Sur, 10 to 15 years of silence and being alone could produce some problems that a little social interaction might heal.

It seems that there have always been people on the margins of society that help keep us a bit more sane, even though they always seem to be a little eccentric. Alan Watts, a popular philosopher in the 50s and 60s, pointed out that there is real value in the psychotic experience to help the rest of us ask the question, "What is reality?" I don't think he was talking about schizophrenia, but alternative lifestyles of people who do not buy into the conventions of the day. The Desert Fathers in Egypt, John the Baptist, Teresa of Avila, and Juan De La Cruz are all noted recluses who avoided the busyness of social conventions to attain a higher spiritual goal. But for the rest of us, living, loving, fighting, loathing and longing for others is our reward and at times our curse in life.

Why All Important Successes Are Social in Nature

Humans are strange creatures when it comes to social connection in so many ways. We all say we value family and celebrate seasons like Thanksgiving and Christmas because they are family times. But then we have a family reunion and come late and leave early and can hardly stand that much exposure to some of our "loved ones." We are nostalgic about small town living but would go postal living where everyone knows your business. We rush into marriages and rush right out again more than half the time.

It seems clear that for most of us our greatest highs and lowest lows involve being with others. If we want more highs than lows, we will need to learn the incredible complexity of social interactions.

We start in life with the instinctual understanding that survival requires social connectedness. Our brains set the stage for social connections when our neurons migrate until they develop a social network with other neurons with which they communicate (Ratey, 2001). We consider ourselves to be the elite creatures on the planet and don't often admit to our instinctive drives. But like all members of the animal kingdom, at birth our instincts drive us to make life-saving connections with our mother and she responds instinctively to care for us until we can care for ourselves (usually somewhere around age 25). The first place we either make it or break it in life is in our family. For those of us whose basic needs are met, we learn to seek out others for pleasure and comfort. Some of us learned that others cannot be counted on; we learned to be suspicious of others and not to rely on them when possible. These are the seeds of social or antisocial orientations to others and to living in a social world.

১৯৬

Bridgette had all the personal attributes, but none of them mattered

Bridgette at age twelve was smart, she was an excellent student, she was healthy, good at sports and activities, she worked hard, was creative, charming, and physically attractive. Oh yes, did I mention that nothing in her life worked? From an early history of severe child abuse, at her young age she found herself in her twelfth placement with no family, no friends, no self-confidence and no hope for the future. With everything Bridgette had going for her, she had one major problem: she could not socially relate to anyone other than her therapist or her teacher. That was it; she was belligerent or intolerably negative with anyone other than a trained adult specifically there to help her and give her undivided attention. Speaking honestly, she only got along with professionals trained to get along with her. Bridgette was an excellent example of having all the raw materials needed by a child for success. However, without the ability to socially connect and relate to others, she was ill prepared to live in a family, get along with peers at school, or live in the community. This one deficit was making all the difference between her success or failure. I can't say what happened in this case because it is still being played out, but without social success in at least limited forms, any other type of success appears to be out of her reach.

࿎ૹ

Fortunately for most of us, social success in our family is facilitated by nurturing adults. Such adults look at wrinkly newborns and say, "Isn't that the cutest baby you have even seen?" I have learned the social convention that this is not a real question and my honest reply of, "Well no, now that you ask" does not lead to a successful social interaction. For nurturing parents, they seem pleased with most everything the infant does. In the early days of a child's life parents are even pleased with a robust full diaper, or a stout belch. When I see parents being proud of their child's crawling, twirling, throwing and most anything else that brings the child attention, I think to myself, "Don't get used to such easy attention, more will be expected of you all the time to gain such praise." And that is exactly what happens. By ages 2 and 3, belching in church is no longer met with praise. A toileting accident is not met with as much pleasantness as it used to. And so it goes; we need to learn the what, where, when, how and with whom of social interactions as we grow older.

The brain is very busy forming around early experiences in life taking place in the family. In fact the brain is more active at this stage in life than at any other time. The evidence suggests that the brain is genetically programmed to be social. This is both an aid to survival and the development of complex mental awareness we call the mind. It appears that the mind develops in our brain because of our interdependence on social connections and our interpersonal relationships (Siegel, 2003). This same mind will begin to play a more expanded role as we mature, and its formation in the early years of family living will go a long way to developing an enduring personality that will travel with us for the rest of our lives.

From the success in the family we head off to school just knowing that everyone there is going to be just as excited about the fact that we are on the planet. However, most of us have the startling discovery that there are other little ones like us that think their antics are just as cute as we think ours are. These other little beings have the nerve to expect adults to meet their every desire just as we expect this. Once again we face the need to understand social conventions or we are in for trouble. There is a great deal to learn about social interactions in kindergarten: taking turns, listening to others, sharing, not grabbing, playing nice, and many more things you often don't observe adults doing in mall parking lots. The social learning curve is steep when we enter school. This may be the reason for the success of the book, *All I Really Need To Know I Learned in Kindergarten* (Fulghum, 1989). But as socially difficult as kindergarten is, we have just started our journey toward social understanding and social proficiency.

There are many measures of success, but when it comes to personal contentment the only successes that matter are social successes. Successes often include: financial security, reaching your career and personal goals, raising and providing for your family, getting the education you desire, and having a healthy, fulfilling life. I will not quibble with any of these. However, we see in our culture that money seldom equates with personal contentment. Climbing the career ladder may or may not mean we feel fulfilled; oftentimes it means we have more stress, more pressure, and more sleepless nights. Reaching our educational goals is a great satisfaction until we see that there is always more to learn and that we now need to use our education to pay the student loans, not to mention the mortgage. Research on personal contentment shows that external gains and accomplishments are great, but they only take us so far.

The successes in life that matter the most to happiness and personal contentment are those related to others. Ask any parent what his or her greatest joy in life is and most will say her partner, her children, and members of her family. Economic level means little unless it helps us provide for those we love, including ourselves. The difference between climbing the corporate ladder and achieving personal contentment has to do with whether you are helping others rather than stepping on others to get ahead. I used to believe that someone needed to be very socially skilled to become a corporate executive. However, recent events in the corporate world have shown us that success at times has meant robbing thousands of investors of their savings to get millions in salaries and bonuses. Little personal contentment comes from getting ahead by harming others along the way.

How Trauma Affects Social Connections and Success

Socialization is very complex and is one of our most difficult challenges growing up. To some this comes naturally. There are gregarious people who make friends easily and are always comfortable with others. Many others are shy and reserved, and the most terrifying experience in their life is standing up in front of the 5th grade class and reciting a poem or giving a report. For traumatized individuals it can be even more challenging, and they often have particular difficulties when it comes to social success. In most cases significant trauma has come at the hands of others. This may result in our not trusting certain people or perhaps anyone. Being gregarious and socially adept is very difficult for people who do not trust others.

Trauma often happens during developmental periods of life where our social skills are affected. When children are concerned with safety, they are less available to learn other important developmental skills. Trauma can affect our comfort level with being in unfamiliar places or being with unfamiliar people. We may be wary of males, or females, or any adults because of bad experiences. Trust is an essential ingredient in social relations. One who has a trust problem, has a social relationship problem. Children, teens and adults can pick up the hesitation and nonverbal discomfort of a lack of trust from someone else. Most of the time these uncomfortable social interactions are avoided and the social distance increases between the individual and others. In this way a social problem has a way of feeding off of itself and getting worse over time. The individual communicates a discomfort around others, others keep their distance, and the individual becomes more ill at ease in social situations.

What Social Success Requires

Life is not a solitary journey; we take every major step in life with others. Ideally, when we are in the presence of others, we feel a connectedness to those around us. For this to be the case, the individual needs to have learned how to connect and bond to another person. A successful bond requires communication, trust, a sense of belonging and a willingness to be vulnerable to someone else. For children who start out in life with the experience of neglect or physical abuse, the experience of vulnerability is contrary to what their brain will naturally want to do. It is the challenge of social connectedness that most seriously impairs a traumatized child's support and social success in life.

On a neurological level, social success requires that two parts of the brain be in agreement. When a person uses executive functions primarily emerging from the frontal lobes of the neocortex, that person decides that to get where he or she wants to go, connections with others are necessary. Simultaneously there is a need to have the limbic system give the go-ahead rather than send warning signals to be wary of others and avoid the vulnerability that is inevitable when we involve someone else in our life. For this neurological synchronisity to take place, the individual needs to have adequately advanced executive development functioning and needs to be free of significant trauma or have healed from past trauma. With this healing, the individual can be aware of the alarms that are being sounded and override them with conscious decisions to do so.

After the individual gets the go ahead from his or her brain, there are still some hurdles to get over. The person needs to have adequate communication skills to get important messages across to others and to receive equally important messages. Over the last ten years in the field of psychology there has been a growing acknowledgment of the importance of emotional intelligence. This can be defined as a way of indicating how the person is able to put cognitive abilities to good use. To a large extent, our emotional intelligence is our ability to negotiate a social world. We must understand our own motives and emotional responses to situations as well as understand those in others. We have long known that communication is 5% words and 95% inflection, cadence, volume, and non-verbal methods of communication. Social success requires success in communicating with others. Communication success requires that we understand the very complex messages we send out and receive back.

We also need a social brain to understand the experience of others. Empathy has been called the highest attainment of the brain, what sets humans apart from all other animals, and what produces the social connectivity that has produced the success of the human species on the planet (Huther, 2006). Recently reported research from the National Institutes of Health has identified parts of the brain that are stimulated by thinking of and helping others. The surprise finding is that the brain appears designed to produce pleasure as a result of empathy in a similar way it produces pleasure in response to food and sex. This fascinating discovery implies that what has been viewed previously as higher-order moral reasoning may actually be quite primitive. It also may indicate that our brains are designed to think of and help others.

Traumatized individuals struggle with communication. It is not as simple as avoiding vulnerability; trauma causes people to either question or misinterpret the motivations and intentions of others. So the person could hear the intended message of, "What do you need?" but interpret the message, "Now what is it and why are you bothering me again?" It is only through a great deal of social interaction that a person improves at communication skills. The irony is that traumatized individuals need these skills more than others, but trauma can get squarely in the way. In frequent social interactions the individual can learn to better understand the intended message of the other person. This is very much a trial-and-error process. However, if a traumatized individual begins to avoid others due to a desire not to take risks, communication skills can suffer greatly. The earlier in life this cycle occurs, the more impactful it will be on the ability of the person to be successful in communication.

Traumatized children are often said to lie frequently. I have always struggled with this assessment because I think it misunderstands the communication of the child. When a child is asked if she knows where the missing remote control is, she is likely to say "No" whether she does or doesn't. This verbal response is often less a matter of deception, an essential ingredient of a lie, than it is an attempt to be careful and not incur someone's anger. What we ask of children, which in part is to understand what we are saying and what we mean, we must also do for them in return. We must use communication that will most effectively state our intent with the traumatized child (or adult). Then we must understand what the child is communicating with 95% of the response, rather than give so much weight to the words. Throughout my career I have found traumatized individuals appreciate it when I overlook their words and hear the truth of their message by their face, their tone, their non-verbal signals and their energy. Only when we do this for them can we help them do this with us and with others.

The study of communication is highly complex and fascinating. Like the human being's ability to walk upright, it is amazing that we develop the ability to truly communicate because of how difficult it is. Last night before going to a fancy party, my wife, Joyce, asked me if the evening dress she was wearing made her backside look odd. Faced with this question, I had to determine accurately the real message she was sending to me and I had to do it fast. Not being in a mood to take a risk (saying what I thought in response), I took the safe approach and asked her to clarify his question. That one exchange was very complex, as most husbands have learned. It was important that I not just consider the words and respond with words. It was critical not to start the evening with a response that could have been misinterpreted.

In psychology we test children by giving them idioms to see if they understand the meaning of a message and not just the words. "A rolling stone gathers no moss," and "A stitch in time saves nine" are not fundamentally about rocks and knitting. However, the person hearing the statement must go deeper than the words. Even more complex are the communications between children at recess, in the hallways of middle school and at school dances in high school. The child who has not learned how to send the message they intend and receive the message that was meant for them is going to be at risk of social mistakes or even failures that become a perpetuating cycle.

The last element to mention here regarding the requirements of social success is a sense of belonging. If a person feels accepted, he or she will generally communicate with others, and if the message does not get through, will try again. However, if the person picks up non-verbal messages that are interpreted as irritation or even hostility, communication will end quickly. I have never visited France, but the French have a reputation of not going out of their way to communicate with visitors unless it is done in precise French. A recent visitor to France told me this has been exaggerated. However, if this was true, the average tourist would likely limit his attempts to communicate when he received an unfriendly reception.

Traumatized individuals often have trouble correctly interpreting the correct message for others. Like the French tourist who does not sense being welcomed, the communication is brief or non-existent. Most of us prefer to feel that the individual we are communicating with is receptive to us and our message. If we mistrust someone, if we have a belief that others are avoiding us, or if someone seems hostile, communication shuts down quickly. Trauma can sometimes leave the individual with trust issues and a habit of misinterpreting a message in a negative direction. Thus, communication is a major issue to address in healing and moving on in a successful way from a traumatic experience.

No Child Is an Island

A baby needs others to survive, a student needs others to learn, an apprentice needs a mentor to become skilled. We cannot avoid the fact that we are inexorably linked to our social network. This is either successfully learned as a very young child or it is not, and the later in life we try to learn this, the harder it is. It has even been proposed that psychosocial competence best describes what the brain is designed for. From this view, the human brain is more asocial organ than even a thinking organ (Huther, 2006).

We learn who we are in relationship to others. Personal insight and self awareness grow from social interactions. It takes some period of time after we are born for us to realize that we are not a part of our mother. We all begin life connected to our mothers, and for most of us we have a lifelong journey attempting to get back to the place of being one with the beloved, either physically in intimate love, emotionally through a heart connection, or spiritually in becoming one with God or the source of life.

But it is not just survival or our need to learn that requires others. We all need social support or else we may survive, but not thrive. This is due to the massive amounts of stress in living and our need to be able to cope with stress. Social support is a major insulating factor from the potentially very negative results of stress.

Stress Inoculation Begins at Birth with Attachment

The first experience we all have in life is that we are dependent on others. No child comes into the world able to fend for him or herself. We all need a care provider, generally our mother, to ensure that we are protected, fed, kept warm, and will have all our basic needs met. Without this critical support, we would all die. As we mature, the stakes may be a bit less life-and-death, but they remain serious. We must have support in life to make it through a maze of threats, challenges, and problems that all come with daily living.

When we instinctively reach out after we are born and our new best friend (our mother) cares for us, we learn quickly to put our needs and our very survival into this person's hands. We learn within a short time to remember this person's smell, her sound, and her face. Within a matter of days we are able to pick Mommy's face out of thousands of other similar faces because we need this face for survival. As we turn over our needs to this person and our needs are promptly met, we are soothed and learn to grow more and more confident in trusting that we will be protected, cared for and loved. In this way we have our physical, emotional and spiritual needs met.

Living is stressful, particularly for those who know they are at the mercy of the environment. However, when the environment is experienced to be safe and nurturing, a child learns to turn the stress arising from basic needs into a relaxed state of comfort. This is where we first experience attachment and the feeling that we are loved and cared for. When this happens the screams arising from the child's basic needs turn into the joyful sounds of bonding with the care provider. Attachment is quickly associated with comfort and stress reduction. This interaction of needs and nurturance forms the basis for a lifetime of social support where we reach out in stress, and through attachment we are comforted and our stress is abated.

The opposite is, of course, also true. The child who screams out to the environment with many basic needs and does not have these needs being met, experiences an increase in stress and soon comes to connect relying on others with increases in unwanted stress. For such children—who have a habit of growing up and becoming adults—attachment does not inoculate against stress, but actually becomes associated with stress. This is why I have previously said that if we can help an individual develop successful attachments in life, we have done more for that person than any other service we could possibly provide.

Research on Social Support

When we start life we have to instinctively rely on the support of others for our very survival. From the very beginning of life, we sink or swim based on the amount of support we receive in meeting our basic needs. As we grow older our basic needs expand beyond protection, touch, nourishment, and warmth. But one thing remains a constant as our needs change: our need for social support remains an important ingredient in first surviving and later thriving in life.

Common sense would tell us that feeling support in life is a good thing. It turns out that feeling support in life is a great thing for a person on multiple levels. We will see in the next chapter that social support in the form of a spiritual community can have a substantial positive impact on the many challenges of living that everyone faces. When we share and find commonality on some of the deeper questions of life, this can be some of the most significant social support we can find in our lives.

Social support from a like-minded spiritual group can be so powerful that it can lead to a cult and a suspension of our most basic needs. The most extreme examples of this are the death cults of Jim Jones, Rev. Moon and Heaven's Gate. Other examples are religious zealots who die in hunger strikes for a cause or blow themselves up for the approval and admiration of others in the jihad. In each of these cases the pull of social support led to an unquestioning allegiance and even a willingness to die to stay within the social group. These are certainly negative extremes that can show the power of our need for social support particularly in our spiritual beliefs. Most of the time social support of a spiritual nature leads to fuller and richer living, where the power of the support is used for positive purposes.

❧❧

Sister Innocence was right all along

In third grade my teacher was a Catholic nun by the name of Sister Mary Innocence (I am not making this up). We aspiring juvenile delinquents of our day referred to her as "Sister Guilty." It turns out that there were several Catholic popes named Innocent, hence the unusual name. Sr. Innocence had to be in her eighties back then, and she is probably still teaching children to this day, at age 136. Anyway, it was Sister's job to help me through a difficult experience one time, and while talking to me she said, "David, always remember that a sorrow shared is halved, but a joy shared is doubled." Fifty years later I have remembered what she said. Now as a psychologist I read research on social support and sharing with others that backs up this statement, and I do my best to share this good news with anyone who will listen. Since she was right about this, I have to wonder if she was also right about the special place in purgatory prepared for students who sassed their teacher in school?

❧❧

We discussed in chapter 7 the research on the physical effects of a positive disposition. In a similar way, social support aids in our positive outlook and one could predict that there are advantages to our physical health. This is exactly what the research indicates.

Perhaps the greatest of possessions is the love of another person. Being loved is even more precious when we consider the research that patients who felt loved had lower levels of coronary arterial sclerosis (Ornish, 1990). Perhaps there is some connection to having a heart full of love and that heart beating longer and better in that state.

A change that I have noticed over the last two decades in hospitals is the switch from rules that are made for the institution to rules that are made to enhance the healing of the patients. One of many examples of this is hospital visiting hours. Visiting a hospital ward was once governed by a rigidly enforced timeline. Now many hospitals have relaxed the times family and supportive visitors can come see the patients. Other hospitals have done away with the restriction on visiting altogether. When medical science learned what enables people to heal faster and need expensive care for shorter periods of time, they began to make practical changes in how the hospital operates.

An example of something that stimulates faster healing was found in a study that social support had a positive effect on surgical recovery and chronic and infectious disease recovery (House, Landis & Umberson, 1988). Surgical recovery rooms are now full of wives, husbands and friends there to help patients get back on their feet faster, and it is working.

Social support must be added to the short list of what helps us to live a better life, experience more happiness and find more personal contentment. Social support is a manifestation of our social success in life. All success in life has a foundation in social success.

THE PATH TO SOCIAL SUCCESS

As we grow older, social interactions become more and more complex.

The successes that matter the most are those that involve other people.

Traumatized individuals often must override internal warnings not to connect with others.

Trauma can impair the person's ability to correctly understand communication.

Successful communication is essential for social success.

Social success is necessary for survival, for learning, and for social support.

Attachment is a key ingredient for social success throughout life.

NINE

SPIRITUAL HEALTH AND LIFE SATISFACTION

The connection between spiritual health and life satisfaction is strong. It is difficult to imagine someone who is very satisfied and fulfilled in life unless such a person possesses a healthy spirit. By the term spiritual I am not speaking only of religion, although religion for many is directly linked with a healthy spirit. The spirit in the context of this chapter is the part of the person that holds the core beliefs, values and principles by which the person lives and makes decisions in life. These are our deepest held beliefs that more than anything else define who we are. If we are unlucky enough to have a physical problem and lose an arm or leg due to disease, we are the same person. If our body changes rapidly and we look entirely different, we are the same person within. This includes the policeman who went into the burning car to save a life and ended up with essentially no facial features and needed multiple reconstructive surgeries. The core of who he was did not change. That which is the most fundamental aspect of who we are, is what I am calling our spirit. From this definition it is easy to see that health of the spirit would involve the individual living a life consistent with his or her core values and principles. When an individual lives in this way, the external rewards, such as praise, economic gain, and status, are minor issues in life satisfaction.

Dave Ziegler

The Professional Bias Against Religion

There has always been an uneasy relationship between religion and the sciences. There have been times in human history where one side or the other has gained the societal power and such times generally resulted in unfortunate excesses by the prevailing side. When religious beliefs hold the power position in a society, the result can be rigid adherence to tradition while ignoring evidence of error. When Galileo presented his scientific position on astronomy that was not consistent with the current thinking, this news was not met with enthusiasm by those holding religious and political power. The result was a suppression of ideas, scientific inquiry being labeled as religious heresy, and the unfortunate scientist reprimanded, imprisoned or worse. At times when science holds the power position, belief and faith are relegated to superstition and ignorance.

Perhaps it is understandable that in the twentieth century, there was a strong negative bias toward religion in many areas of science, including psychology. The move away from religious dogma influencing science became so strong that religious or spiritual belief was often viewed as opposed to science, or that science could justifiably say that spiritual belief had no role in the discussion of health and healing.

In the field of psychology, I am not sure when the anti-religious bias was the strongest. But I can relate a couple of personal experiences. In my early twenties I was facing a change in my plans for a career. It was a challenging time, but I was engaged with life and enjoying myself although I had sufficient internal confusion to seek some outside help. I was able to find a counselor who had professional and religious experience to work with me over a period of several months. This ex-minister was very helpful when I discussed my struggles and my feelings as long as they did not directly relate to my spiritual beliefs. At first I picked up the subtle signs that he would change the subject if I raised a spiritual struggle. After awhile I asked him why he did not want to discuss with me how my internal struggle related to a career that for me had to include my spiritual beliefs. He responded that if I insisted on talking about spiritual issues, he could not help me and would refer me to someone else. Faced with what was to me a clear statement of my counselor's problem, I took him up on his offer to refer me elsewhere.

In the late 60s and early 70s I noticed striking animosity from psychology toward religious and spiritual issues. This came out in classes I took, in books I read, and in attitudes of students and faculty when I was in undergraduate and graduate school. A poignant experience occurred in 1971 when I joined a therapy group. There were eight members plus a psychologist who facilitated the group. The initial session of the group was memorable. After the ground rules were explained to everyone and we made our commitments to confidentiality, we all discussed why we had decided to join the group and what we wanted out of the experience. One member was hurt and angry from a recent divorce, another was depressed about challenges with her parents, and each of the participants had their turn. When it came to me, I told the group that my life was going reasonably well but I was trying to adjust from the spiritual beliefs I had been taught growing up and now trying to develop my own beliefs about life, meaning and purpose, and where God fit into this for me. Before I spoke, I was encouraged that regardless of the issue raised by the participants the facilitator listened well and was encouraging to the individual and invited others to add supportive input. However, as I spoke I could not help but notice a growing anxiety in the behavior and reactions of the group. To my surprise I was stopped before I was finished and the facilitator asked the group if they wanted religious issue to be a part of the group. The group voted 7 to 1 (guess who the one was) to disallow any issues related to religion or spiritual issues. I was both shocked and amazed. Although I pursued other resources to meet my specific needs, I stayed in the group. It soon was disclosed that two of the participants were ex-religious (a minister and a nun) and five other members were raised in strict religious traditions that they now completely rejected. Even the facilitator had once studied for the ministry. It was clear to me that the members of this group had not done their own internal work in the areas I wanted to discuss and they collectively wanted to keep it that way.

This therapy group is representative of the attitude that was once strong in psychology related to religious and spiritual issues. This attitude can still be found, but much less than in the past, and for good reason. Due to the many influences on the mental health of an individual, it is absurd to attempt to categorize a person by putting the physical aspect over here, the emotional over there, and the spiritual over in the corner. At the deepest level of who we are can be found our spiritual self; from this place comes our inner working model of the world and how we believe things work. From here we develop our emotional dispositions toward the world around us. At the deepest level we cannot separate our emotions, our thoughts and our bodies, they become one. How could someone explore the psychology of any individual without giving attention to the beliefs and values that make up the person?

While the professional bias against religion has vastly improved, there remain those who see the clouds in the silver lining (Exline, Yali & Sanderson, 2000; Sloan, Bagiella & Powell, 2001). However the vast majority of scientific study on the subjects of religion, spirituality and physical and mental health indicates that the thoughts, beliefs and behaviors associated with core spiritual beliefs lengthen the lifespan and enhance the individual in a wide variety of ways (McCullough, Hoyt, Larson, Koenig & Thoresen, 2000).

Religion Has Been in the Power Position Longer Than Science

Part of the reason for the bad attitude of science toward religion is that in the battle between the two, and there have definitely been battles, religion has been in the catbird seat for more time than science. It still irritates astronomers to think of how Galileo, Copernicus and many other scientists were silenced by the Church. But such battles are not in the past. We now have raging differences over issues such as stem cell research, when a zygote becomes a human being, whether creationism fits into the science text books and other religion vs. science controversies.

In some ways over the last fifty years the pendulum has swung in the other direction. For some time science has been in the power position over belief and religion. Perhaps the pinnacle of this time was the late sixties. Problems are created when the pendulum swings to either extreme. When we look to dogma and beliefs to inform us of the physical universe we end up with Rome being the center of the universe. However, when we look to science to guide our way we end up with some of the abuses of Nazi Germany and with atomic, chemical and biological weapons that our country tries to keep other countries from developing though we have each of them ourselves. These are weapons that reflect an incredible absence of moral responsibility to conceive, design, build and maintain as an unspeakable threat to living beings everywhere. We cannot have scientists running our society any more than we can have generals running our government, or for that matter bishops or mullahs. There is a place in our society for the soldier and the scientist, but these roles must be informed by the philosopher, the ethicist, and the clergy.

The more we learn in science the more some of our beliefs start making surprising sense. I am fascinated by the fact that the Biblical story of Adam and Eve is looking more credible all the time. Recent announcements from the National Geographic Society's DNA research indicate that there very well may have been an Eve who is the mother of all Homo Sapiens. Advancements in DNA technology are allowing us to go back to the routes of mankind and track origins and migrations over thousands of years. So are we all related and offspring of a common mother? DNA science is now suggesting what the Bible has long told us—yes, it is looking like we all have a common mother.

We may be wise enough at this point to prevent pendulum swings that neglect science for religion or religion for science. Each can better inform the other, although both are essentially different disciplines that often ask very different questions. One thing is for sure, we cannot divorce our emotions or our psychological health from our values and beliefs. Our psychological health is closely linked to our spiritual health.

What Is Spiritual Health?

A brief definition of spiritual health could be that we see our core beliefs manifested in the decisions we make in life. Perhaps the opposite of spiritual health is spiritual illness, or when we internally agonize over the absence of our beliefs being reflected in the way we live. It is not a coincidence that the most effective approaches ever found to treat addictions have been twelve-step programs. One way of describing these programs is that they are spiritually based methods of becoming attuned to core beliefs. Addictions of all types are manifestations of a lack of internal balance, and following a prescribed method to get back to core beliefs helps to regain balance once again.

It makes sense that some of our strongest and deepest

beliefs have a very powerful influence over our state of health. There are many examples of people who suffered for their beliefs and yet had some superhuman ability to endure hardship. Nelson Mandela comes to mind here. At the same time there are other examples where an individual loses hope and a reason to go on, and this can be followed by either a rapid or slow demise. My experience working with people in the dying process has shown me that a person's will to live has a profound impact on how long the heart keeps pumping and the lungs keep expanding. The will to live seems to be integrally linked to physical survival.

Because of the important role played by spiritual beliefs and spiritual health in physical survival, spiritual issues come into play in resiliency. It would make sense that individuals who have a foundation rooted in spiritual beliefs and spiritual health would show more resiliency. This has been borne out in research where individuals with a strong religious or spiritual belief system were shown to have multiple advantages over those who do not, including: having less depression, less anxiety, better coping styles and better responses better to illness, divorce and bereavement. Once again the link between facing adversity and spiritual beliefs can easily be seen. If a person is facing the death of a loved one and has a belief that the person is now in a better place, this is going to impact the bereavement process in a positive way. Or if someone is fighting an addiction to alcohol, and believes in placing his trial in the hands of a higher power, this may constitute the best type of support system available.

The internal support people feel from spiritual beliefs can be significant. An underlying value that exists in most spiritual belief systems is the awareness of connectedness with all things. This includes a sense of connection to loved ones who are not physically with us, to other members of a belief system, and perhaps to all human beings or all of creation. It is hard to be lonely if you have a spiritual sense of being connected with everything around you. When such a person becomes ill, putting this problem in the hands of God and believing that this will make a difference often results in a difference taking place.

అంఈ

Where did the cancer go?

A number of years ago I took all my cars to a young mechanic. He was good at what he did with cars and was also in night school to finish a college degree. One day he approached me in a very somber way and said I would have to find another mechanic. I was stunned and asked why. With tears in his eyes he told me of his physical ordeal over the last month where he noticed a problem that was diagnosed by his doctor as an aggressive form of terminal cancer. He was told that there was little they could do and to put his affairs in order. Telling me this was for him part of him not leaving people without a mechanic when he was gone. Not a strong religious person before his diagnosis, he became very involved in a church. He called me three months later and asked if I had found another mechanic; I had not. He sounded great, and I asked him how he was doing. His excited answer was that God had cured him. He related that with his and others' prayers he did not deteriorate as expected and began to slowly improve. When his cancer did not continue its aggressive course his doctor did further checks and found no sign of any cancer in his system. The doctor had no explanation, but the patient did: his spiritual beliefs had saved his physical body. His doctor said that was a better explanation than he was able to provide. Many years later the cancer has never returned.

࿋

As a student of individuals who have been known to excel in the spiritual realm, I have been interested in the fact that spiritual health at times does not bring physical or psychological health. When we look at great men who have strong spiritual convictions, we don't always find individuals who lived a long and satisfying life. Such individuals as Jesus, Francis of Assisi, Gandhi, Siddhartha Gautama (Buddha), Mohammad, Abraham Lincoln and Martin Luther King are all examples of very principled individuals who had less time on the planet as a result of sharing and living those principles. It seems that we are not likely to be fully healthy individuals without spiritual health, but living by our spiritual principles can also at times be hazardous to our health.

How the Spirit Touches All Aspects of the Individual

Because the spirit involves our deepest held values and beliefs, it influences every aspect of ourselves. We have seen above where spiritual health can help with physical health and vice versa. In the same way spiritual connectedness can help with our emotional and psychological health. Spiritual strength helps us to handle adversity and even spend years in prison unfairly punished for taking a principled stance. We saw how their spiritual beliefs helped the Amish parents grieve for the loss of their children to a deranged gunman, and they then demonstrated superhuman strength to forgive the gunman and send support and help to the gunman's family.

How does someone become cured of cancer through prayer? How does someone confined in a jail cell for twenty long years not give up? These are answers that as yet confound our scientific explanations, but it appears that we are getting closer to having at least partial answers. We now have science that points to the importance of support to our ability to cope with adversity. We also have science that links our spiritual beliefs to how we handle stress, anxiety, adversity, death, disappointment and losses of all kinds. It may be that we are close on a material level to explaining some of the miraculous events that have always been a part of medicine and psychology. What we may never have proof of is the spiritual power of prayer itself and of God's intervention in our lives. But just knowing the advantages in life of people who have a well-developed spiritual belief system that they put into practice and live by could be ample motivation to become one of these people. The next section takes a closer look at these advantages.

Some are more familiar with the term soul than spirit. It could be said that what the mind is to the brain, the soul is to the body. The soul is the life principle, the place of depth that makes every person not only a unique individual but a distinctive footprint in both the material and spiritual universe. As we must acknowledge and care for the mind if we want to achieve personal contentment, so must we care for the soul. Some years ago, Thomas Moore wrote what could be described as an owner's manual for the soul in the book *Care of the Soul* (1992). Moore advocates re-looking at the role the soul plays in our lives including meaning, imagination, humor, depth and playfulness. The soul houses the sacred in our lives, and without the sacred we have neither psychological nor spiritual health. Caring for the soul brings the intrapersonal witness to events in our lives, both significant and mundane. The soul can guide a person to mental health, and in fact was the primary means to do so before the modern era of reliance on psychotherapy. The soul allows, absorbs, forgives, understands, and aligns itself with wisdom that often goes far beyond the individual. A life devoted to soulful living is behind the wisdom of every major religious tradition. However, relying upon the rules, dogmas, and external rituals without understanding the soul or depth of any tradition is the source of fanaticism. It is fanaticism that has given religion a well-deserved bad name at times throughout history, including our own.

A life lived in the spirit, or an existence focused on the care of the soul, can be every bit as direct a route to personal contentment as any amount of study, coaching, or psychotherapy.

The Research on Spiritual Health and Life Satisfaction

It is important to say from the outset that research does not account for individual differences. Statistical sampling does not hold true for the entire population. You will find miserable people who are members of the fraternal organization known as the Optimists. You will find well-adjusted and spiritually healthy people who do not believe in God and have never set foot in a church. However, research does make some generalizations about large numbers of people who represent populations. For this reason the findings of social research are well worth considering.

Being religious is not always the same thing as being spiritual, although it is for many people. However, both religious and spiritual people appear to share similar advantages in life. Starting with people who belong to a religion or faith community, this affiliation appears to help the individual in multiple ways. For example, we know that social support is a critical factor in handling life stress and adding to our ability to manage our lives. People who are active in a religious faith community have greater social support than those who do not. Even Karl Marx, who called organized religion "the opium of the people," would have to admit that connection to a religious community enhances a person's ability to cope with the world and not just deaden the pain.

Research on happiness indicates that three factors play the most significant role in internal happiness. The first is pleasure. Although this has the least influence of the three factors leading to happiness, pleasure is a good thing most of the time and helps to make us happier. The second is much more important, and it is engagement. The more we are involved in what is going on around us, the more fulfilled, needed, and happy we are. But the third and greatest contributor to happiness is finding meaning and purpose in our lives. The greater of the three of these factors is directly linked with being involved in a religious community of believers.

But the advantages do not end there. Religion opens itself to being criticized by those who reject the many rules involved in the moral code of religions. Many people reject the "thou shalt not..." approach to living. They argue that what we do is much more important than what we don't do. Perhaps the greatest criticism of religious Christians is that they go to church and pretend to be holy and then leave church to live a life that involves cheating people, fighting to get ahead in business with unethical behavior, and doing little to help their fellow man. In other words, the criticism is that many Christians are hypocrites. Christianity or any other religion does not have a corner on the hypocrisy market. But the negative view of the rules of religion ignores one very important thing, that when religion provides rules to live by this simplifies the lives of followers and helps them to make better decisions, including the avoidance of serious risk-taking behaviors.

There is some logic to the following findings of social research:

- Faith in a higher power has been consistently linked to life satisfaction. It seems that if someone has a lifelong belief in a benevolent God who watches over the person and provides faith and hope for the journey of life, such a person will have psychological advantages over someone without this inner working model of living.

- Religion provides people with a buffer toward the stress of life. It is interesting how religion helps with handling stress. In some ways it would seem that guilt in sinful acts could increase the stress of living. But nearly all religions have a method of realigning with the fold and with God. If the person follows the tenets of the religion, these is a sense of confidence about the decisions that he is making, and in most cases there are some promises of rewards in both the afterlife and right here in this life.

- Religious practices of all types have been linked to frequent positive emotions and overall satisfaction in life. When many people take the time to go to a church, synagogue or mosque and pray with others in beautiful buildings designed to lift our spirits, is it any mystery that our spirits are often lifted? The message of all religions is that life is not random, there is a plan and a purpose, though we just may not see it clearly. These messages are affirming, they are comforting, and in a life filled with many threats and bad experiences, positive feelings associated with meaning and purpose assist with happiness in life.

- Compassion, as preached by religions, is linked to happiness in life. The seeming paradoxes of most religious principles are exactly what imparts their value to many people. The law of the asphalt jungle is to get them before they get you. To love our enemies and do good to those who hurt us is so illogical that to do so successfully aligns us with a higher order and more heavenly plane. To love, to give, to help and to follow, for example, the Christian beatitudes, brings a level of meaning and purpose that feels almost otherworldly. Many of us allow ourselves this experience during the holiday season. Giving to the hungry, clothing the naked, giving drink to the thirsty, visiting prisoners, and other acts of compassion help us to live the grace of God and participate in our religious beliefs in a way that feeds the spirit deeply and adds immeasurably to happiness.

- People who believe in an afterlife are generally happier than those who do not. This is perhaps the easiest of these principles and their resulting consequences to understand. Even people who do not believe in an afterlife often express that they wish they could. It seems only logical to most of us that working hard and learning in fourth grade will allow us further opportunities in the fifth grade. If so, how could it make sense that after a full life of struggle it would all just end in a final gasp? The people who do not struggle with this issue and simply believe in a continuation of life are those who are happier than those who do not hold this belief.

Reality and Quantum Physics

I feel compelled to get somewhat philosophical and complicated for a short visit to the world of quantum mechanics. It may be complex, but the information brings with it an important perspective in our discussion of reality. If this sounds more complicated that you are interested in, then jump to the next section, but I hope you do not. The reason I believe it is important to include this discussion in this book is that the world of quantum mechanics is the world we live in, it is just that most of us don't know this yet. Read on and you will be one of the quickly growing but small number of people who have been exposed to quantum mechanics.

I must ask you to stick with me on this to the end, I promise to make some sense of some wildly confusing ideas. Let me start with what quantum physics is. Briefly stated, quantum physics, somewhat interchangeable with quantum mechanics, is the study of possibilities in the physical universe with particular interest in the subatomic structure of matter (Goswani, 2004). And what, might you ask, does that have to do with a book on moving beyond healing and finding personal contentment in life? It turns out that this subject has a great deal to do with the focus of this book. The reason for this is that not only are psychology and theology very interested in our personal influence on our subjective reality, but they are also interested is one of the most traditionally mechanized physical sciences — physics. I believe we can learn from what is presently going on in the exploding world of quantum physics.

The issues and research going on in this part of physics are so convoluted and mind boggling that it is surprising that it is receiving so much attention. Part of the reason for quantum physics becoming of interest to a wide audience was a Hollywood movie with the irritating name of *What The Bleep Do We Know* (Arntz, W., Chasse, B. & Hoffman, M., 2004). This independent film with a confusing premise and alternative style has been something of a sleeper hit. It is a mixture of some Hollywood graphics and flashy photography, interspersed with interviews by an assortment of scientists, philosophers, medical and psychology professionals, and even a psychic for good measure. See this movie when you get the opportunity (it is available in DVD). I want to touch on some of the premises highlighted in the movie and expand just a bit on them.

- What we commonly refer to as "reality" turns out to be more complex than we have previously believed. We know from anthropology that our perceptions of reality are embedded in cultural understandings. For example, there are primitive cultures with no understand of shapes such as triangles or squares because these shapes don't exist in nature or the culture they have built. The question becomes do we influence how we experience our objective reality, or is our experience reality? This has been a very challenging question for philosophers for hundreds of years since Descartes' statement, "I think, therefore I am." Physicists have now leaped into the arena of what is reality and what is consciousness, and they are coming up with some surprising findings.

- The deeper physicists go into the subatomic physical world, the more questions they come up with and the fewer answers they find. Physicists have always been different than philosophers, since physics is grounded in the material world rather than the world of ideas, but this is no longer true. The distinction between the physical world and the world of thought, ideas and consciousness itself is fading away.

- There are many theories, but the world of subatomic particles confounds our understanding and even flies in the face of our beliefs about the mechanistic physical universe. As the ability of the physicist to go further into the subatomic level of matter expands the Newtonian, mechanistic and mathematical explanations of matter are not only being revised, they are being replaced. Previous understandings do not explain what is being discovered.

Hang in there, I am still building a case here.

- Matter is not static and predictable at its foundations. All branches of science have viewed the material world as real, stable, and predictable, and the physical laws of the universe as static and unchanging. The best I could explain the current change in thinking is to say that this premise is now the equivalent to the "scientific knowledge" that the universe revolved around the earth once was an accepted fact. Physicists are not finding static or predictable qualities of matter as they go deeper into this tiny world of the foundations of the material universe. In fact the distinction between the world of matter and the world of ideas is now being questioned.

- At the subatomic level, matter is more of a thought than a substance in part because all matter goes in and out of our plane of existence. You read that right, the mechanistic principles of Newtonian physics appear not to apply to the building blocks of matter. You will still read in physics textbooks the principle of conservation of matter — matter can neither be created nor destroyed, it can only be changed. Particularly for us busy people with multiple meetings at the same time, we all know that matter, such as our bodies, cannot be in more than one place at the same time. Oh yeah? Then what is going on when subatomic particles come into and go out of existence constantly. They also have a rude habit of being in multiple physical places at the same time. There is a name for this: quantum superposition.

- Quantum superposition means that matter is in many places at the same time but when we subjectively focus on it, it collapses into one location. I realize all this may be sounding a little crazy, just what is going on? The current answer from physicists is that we just don't know, but the possibilities may be leading to the most exciting scientific discoveries of all time. Early indications appear to point to the fact that the difference between the observer (us) and the physical world we observe (objective reality) may not be illusory. The key appears to be our brain. Now we are getting back to the topic of this book.

- Our brains play a substantial role not only in our subjective experience but also in our objective reality. We have known for a very long time that we can influence how we feel by what we think. As one of many positive potentials of human beings, our ability to affect our subjective experience has not reached its full potential in most people. Now we hear from physical science that our brains may also play a major role in the objective reality around us. Can we change everything by our own internal power of mind — the evidence is mounting that this is the case. So if you want to change your feelings, change the way you think. And if you want to change your reality, again, change the way you think.

- We bring all physical matter into reality by our consciousness. We create our external reality when we create our internal reality. For thousands of years philosophers have asked questions such as what is reality, and who, where, and why are we here, and by the way where is here? Quantum physics is now embracing these questions mainly because what they are finding about matter requires them to do so. They are still at the theory level, but the greatest commonality in the many theories about all this is that we create physical matter around us by collapsing many potentials into one reality by the way we focus our conscious awareness.

- There is a direct influence of our thoughts on our outside reality as well as our internal reality. We create both the internal and the external world that we live in. If you have stayed with me to this point and you are saying to yourself that all this is just too weird, you are not alone. What is going on? It is too soon to say, but it does appear that, "Toto, I don't think we are in Kansas anymore."

- The inescapable conclusion from physics, and not just from psychology, is that we create the reality we live in. So if you are like me and don't yet understand how our minds create the chair we are sitting on, or the movie we are watching, or the car we are driving down the freeway 10 miles over the speed limit, it may not be necessary to have lunch with Steven Hawking to figure it out. But we can acknowledge that the distinctions between the "hard sciences" (chemistry, physics and mathematics), and the "soft sciences" (philosophy and psychology) are rapidly blurring. But before I do what I promised, to make some sense out of all this, there is more, actually there is much more to explain.

When there is a breakthrough in science, many premises can shift, and this can produce a major change in the paradigm that guides our thinking and our scientific inquiry. When physicists found that subatomic particles did not adhere to our understanding of the physical rules of matter, they had to come to the conclusion that we now need new rules. This finding has also opened up other aspects of our paradigm for closer study. For example, quantum physics is now leaning in the direction of our subjective consciousness originating from outside rather than inside our brain. What was that, our brains create the world we experience and our mind comes from outside of us? This is starting to hurt my head, but let's go just a little further.

Stuart Hameroff, M.D., is a doctor of anesthesiology and a researcher on what consciousness is. He observes people being anesthetized and wonders where the mind goes during this time. His understanding of medicine and quantum physics leads him to have no quarrel with saying that there is evidence of a person's spirit, or soul. He also has no problem with the new paradigm being explained by the concept of God (Hameroff, 2003). We may have come full circle. We may now be observing the foundations of the physical world and learning that the mental, physical and spiritual components of existence are all joined and interrelated, and there may be growing scientific findings that can be interpreted to point to God being behind it all.

Bear with me for one more step into the strange world of a new paradigm that no one yet understands. Nancy Woolf, Ph.D., is a neuroscientist. Her specialization is in the study of how the brain uses neurotransmitters, specifically acetylcholine. Her research is finding yet another convergence with some of the above issues. At the fundamental level of chemical operations in the receptors of the brain, classical views of neurobiology fail to explain what is going on and the explanations of quantum computations is reflecting a better explanation. Specifically the rich data in the chemical transfers in the brain collapse into a cohesive message that can be understood and passed on (Woolf, N.J., 2003). From our discussions of how the brain operates, this explanation may provide us with a possible explanation of how our brain could possibly create our external reality.

But enough with all the complexity; what does it all mean to a person trying to heal from trauma and move on in life? I will do my best to answer this question.

When we consider the strange world of quantum physics, now we have multiple possibilities that we face. The rock we hold in our hand is not solid, it is made up of particles that disappear randomly so that without our brain focusing on the rock, it is not a rock but multiple potentials. We also have quantum physics providing a possible answer to how billions of chemical transfers result in anything our brain's can use, rather than a cacophony of random noise. We have physical scientists finding explanations in spiritual realities and even a growing paradigm that implies a connectedness to consciousness, the unity of the spirit in all people, the external source of the mind, and the concept of God as explanation for it all. Wow! But why have I included all this in this book?

For many people it is not enough to say, "Don't worry, be happy." It is also not enough to say, "Always look on the bright side of your life." We have had such simplistic platitudes floating around our culture for a long time. It is not that these expressions are not good ideas, in fact they are very good ideas, but why? The reason it is important to consider our own internal power to affect what goes on in our mind, body and spirit is that we are now learning from many directions that either you take charge of your experience, your thoughts, your feelings and your world, or you leave it to other influences such as past traumas to determine the quality of your satisfaction in life and your personal contentment.

I have brought together the current research and thinking in positive psychology, philosophical/spiritual premises, and the emerging thinking of physics to show that these disciplines are coming up with not only the same questions, but also the same answers. To the question of who we are and why we are, the answer is something like: we are conscious beings who are connected to other conscious beings in a way similar to how neurons in our brain are connected to others and form a collective entity. We are also defined by our consciousness and on what we choose to focus.

For a moment consider the implications coming from the hard science, quantum physics. What if the theory turns out to be correct that there is no difference between what is within us and what is outside of us (Wolf, 1989)? Our brains determine our experience, and our brains take their leads from an interconnectedness with a collective consciousness, not unlike one computer connected to others all over the world, resulting in what we call the internet. (By the way, that idea was viewed as preposterous just a few years ago.) Our reality actually is "the" reality. This would help explain some of the research in near-death experience, as one example—why some people "die" and are met by a loved one, Buddha, Jesus, or a demonic spirit. Each person determined their own near-death experience, although there was some commonality to other people's experiences.

That we determine our own experience would also help explain why people who think negative thoughts live in a negative world with more sadness, more physical dis-ease and shorter lifespans. In the same way this could help explain why optimistic and positive people have and feel more support, enjoy greater success in all areas, have fewer accidents and heal quicker from illness, among the many aspects of the positive reality they create.

The philosopher in me cannot resist taking this issue of our inner and outer reality one step further. If there is no difference between our internal and external reality, meaning that we create both, then what about God and creation? As Stuart Hameroff (2003) explains, this theory does not preclude the existence of God. Stated briefly, God may be the consciousness that imparts the mind in each brain. If this is the case, what about life choices and free will? It occurs to me that God may have set up the material world to intersect with the spiritual world in the brain/ mind components of the human body. Perhaps free will is our ability to create our own inner as well as outer reality. The implications are fascinating to say the least, as well as the fact that theology has Physics to thank for this theory.

From this discussion there are several important points. First, none of us are really alone. We talked about the new findings from anthropology that we can all trace our pasts to the same mother and thus are all relatives. Our consciousness appears to have its beginnings outside of our subjective self, from a collective or spiritual consciousness, and this is coming from a hard science, physics. We also determine who we are and what goes on around us. We are growing in our understanding that we are indeed the director of our own play and the author of our own life story. This is not to say that we do not run into challenging or undesirable things in our created world. But the power of any experience, or any person, place or thing rests on our mind and how we want to integrate what we encounter in life. We decide what is "real"; we decide if our world is a nightmare or a wonderful adventure. This is not only true of our psychological self and our spiritual self, but it is also appears to be true of our material self.

So with these new puzzle pieces to add to our billion-piece puzzle, the picture is still difficult to fully see, but we have glimpses that are important for us to integrate into our understanding. One of the most important sections of the puzzle coming into focus is how we do indeed create our world — our mind, our body, our spirit and the world around us.

Creating Our Reality

Whether we listen to quantum physicists, Eastern spiritual teachers, or the psychology of affirmations, there is growing evidence that we have the ability to create our own reality. From taking charge of an experience to changing what is going on around us, there appears to be formidable ways that we can shape our reality.

During dinner last night we were sitting down to eat when one of the grandchildren had a quarrel with the other. There was a scratch and then a kick and then tears. The older of the two, who did the retaliatory kick, immediately and ineffectively proclaimed her complete innocence, while communicating quite the opposite in her energy. She put herself into a time-out in a bedroom and cried and screamed that life was unfair. I was intrigued by this display that on the surface seemed to have little external significance. It was not a serious incident and no consequences were needed. I find that children have internal processes similar to adults, but children are more honest in expressing their thoughts and emotions. This child was screaming that she did nothing as if she could either change reality or talk herself into how she would like to change the situation she found herself in. Of course, the irony was that the keys to changing her reality were within her during the entire period of her 20 minute outburst, and it was only herself that she needed to convince.

I see some parallels in this extended outburst based upon how this young child perceived a situation and the lives of most adults. In the above situation, the child convicted herself as guilty of an offense, and she made it more serious than it was. She then punished herself based upon this self judgment. Next, she believed that a loud and extended reaction would somehow make the situation better when in fact it was this response to the internal perception itself that actually caused the problem she was having in the first place. The parallel is that adults do this frequently, though they usually are better able to hide the more embarrassing aspects of the reactivity. Although there are some exceptions to adults internally hiding a very childish reactivity — Michael Richards' and Mel Gibson's racist rants come to mind — most of us struggle internally in a similar way that my granddaughter externally struggled with last night.

We first perceive a situation and immediately determine that our perception is reality. This may or may not be true, oftentimes our perception is just that, our internal meaning that we affix to a situation. Then we add our judgment to the event, who was right, who was at fault, who was insensitive, who was justified. All of these determinations are completely subjective. Many times we see that we are at fault in the situation. Our childish nature would like to change the reality of the situation by denial, argument, or even throwing a tantrum to see if that might work. Our emotional reactivity seldom changes our internal perception, and like my granddaughter, we end up reacting to our own perceptions and end up squarely in our own way to feeling better about the situation.

❧❦

He demanded input into the storyline of his life.

When it comes to discussing the concept of creating your own reality and being the author of your story, it is difficult to come up with a better example than Lance Armstrong. He was mentioned in Chapter Three but he deserves further mention for his completely changing the course of his life through willpower. He could have placed his entire focus on healing from cancer, then took it easy as his doctors recommended, and no one would have thought less of him. He wanted more and demanded more of his sick body and his prognosis in life. It could have turned out that the cancer beat him rather than he beating it, but he would have gone down a competitor. As it turned out, his cancer was an opportunity for Lance to change his thinking, his emotions, and his spirit, and in the process he has dramatically changed the lives of many people around the world. What is a bigger accomplishment, giving people a model for willing themselves well and then willing themselves a champion, or finishing first in a series of bicycle races?

❧❦

This is a simplistic example of more complex dynamics that happen in the lives of adults all the time. The dynamics in our jobs, the struggle of needs and desires in our intimate relationships, and the complexity of our relationships with our parents, our children and members of our families are all places where we find the most challenge to impacting what goes on around us. It is a natural instinct to want to have some control over what goes on in our lives. On a primitive level, control aids survival. There are several places in the example of the tantrum where many individuals look in all the wrong places to have some control over their experience.

The first way we can have more control over what goes on in our lives is to realize that our internal subjective experience becomes our objective reality. When we learn this we open ourselves to the subjective observations of others and really listen to explanations other than our own about what has happened. In this way we can change our reality if we don't like the one we have. Our next control could come in how we judge the situation. We frequently have a faulty assessment of the importance of an event or our role in the event. Being open to alternative explanations and input from other sources is a major way that we can have more control over the internal meaning we give to events. We can then respond to an event rather than react to it. Responses are more volitional, more thoughtful, and less emotional and reactive. How many times do we make a bad situation worse with our reactivity? When we find ourselves unable to get out of the rut "others put us in," we may want to consider that the rut in which we find ourselves has much more to do with our internal experience than what others are doing. At each of the above points, we can change the reality of our lives by changing our internal thoughts about the situation.

The saying, "Change yourself and you change the world," is rooted in science. We can indeed change most anything in life by internally changing how we perceive, how we judge and how we decide to respond to the situation. If we all did an internal assessment of the greatest difficulties we face in life, I think we would find that these are also the places where we demonstrate the greatest mental rigidity.

We make our life either harder or easier by the way we think and feel about the situations we find ourselves in.

Healthier people have a wider range of strategies to accomplish a goal through one door, and if it is locked to back up and go through a different door. Healthier people use their ability to create their own reality to prevent going too far down a one-way street and being unwilling to back up and try another route. We have seen that optimists influence their life experience in a much more positive way than pessimists do, and wouldn't all of us like to have a more positive life?

These lessons in how to create our own reality in a more positive and satisfying direction are particularly important when it comes to those responding to serious traumatic experiences. For these individuals there are more hurdles to jump and higher mountains to climb in order to attain personal contentment. Whether you are someone bouncing back from serious trauma or just one of the six billion members of the human family, how we use our mental faculties has a great deal to do with the quality of our lives and the nature of our experiences. The power is in our hands, or more, precisely, in our brains, to change ourselves, and to change the world. Now *there* is some real control.

THE PATH TO LIFE SATISFACTION

Satisfaction is linked to and requires a healthy internal spirit.

Our spirit contains our beliefs, our values, and what makes us who we are.

Spiritual health is when our core beliefs are manifest in our life.

Spiritual health requires attunement to our core beliefs.

Spiritually healthy people are more resilient.

What affirms our spirit also brings life satisfaction.

We create both our internal reality and our external reality.

Ten

Prescriptions For A Better Life

I must admit to some hesitation in starting this chapter. Pick up any magazine at the newsstand and you will find articles on the ten ways to happiness, or at least to a more fulfilled sex life. I have to explain what I see as the difference between those magazines and this chapter. The difference is science. The issues that I will raise here are grounded in psychology and have been informed by multiple scientific studies to provide solid ways to make a positive difference in your life. However, feel free to go ahead and buy the magazine and improve your sex life if you wish.

I don't plan to share any great revelation to conclude this book. These are not secrets that have been buried under a bristlecone pine for the last six thousand years. In fact, if you find in this chapter anything other than common sense I would expect you to be surprised. We have access to a great deal of information in our modern world. Subsequently, if we read even occasionally, we will be exposed to considerable information about living and having a better life.

Locally, we even have a radio station with a mission to help its listeners be successful in life. This is not generally what I expect of a radio station, but I appreciate the effort. Is having a good life really that hard, that we have to get so much help along the way? Since man has walked the planet,

I think the answer is yes, life is that difficult, and any help along the way is a plus.

Information comes to us in all forms of media about better living. At times the only thing we need to be careful of is to determine if the information is designed to sell us something or not. If it is, then buyer beware. There is no end to the marketing of products that are disguised as news, scientific announcements, and even research. But with just a little looking, any computer with internet access can tune you into information on a national and international scale that would have Galileo, da Vinci and even Einstein spellbound.

We can move a computer mouse and find the results of most federally funded research on our health — most of which is like this chapter, just good common sense. We know that in our diet fiber is good and animal fat is bad. We know that green leafy vegetables are a better source of nutrition than the most often eaten vegetable in America, the french fry. We know that exercise is good and a sedentary life is bad for your health. So if we know all this already, why do we need a new type of diet every few months so that people can recommit to living in a more healthy and lean fashion? The answer appears to be that we don't really use what we know in order to change our habits of living. Since this appears to be true for eating, exercise, stress management and keys to a happy life, the odds may be low that this chapter will have the results intended: to provide ideas that readers will use to enhance their personal contentment through the way they choose to live.

There is no doubt that we are one of the most curious members of the animal kingdom. We do so many things that defy logic. We worry about the safety of air travel (at least I do), but we hurry to the airport in our car and in so doing are 1,000 times more likely to seriously injure ourselves. We focus on the color of the national threat level, but we are more likely to drown in the bathtub than die at the hands of a terrorist. While many people worry about unseen threats, one out of every five adults embraces one of life's most serious threats: smoking. Twenty percent of adults in this country continue to smoke cigarettes, a practice that ends up killing 1,500 men, women and children every day of the year, or the same loss of life as the September 11th tragedy every other day. I will have to leave it up to you, whether you will really listen to any of the ideas I cover in this chapter to improve your happiness and open up new avenues to personal contentment.

What Does Not Improve Our Life

Before going into what does improve our lives, perhaps it would be good to say a few things about what does not improve our lives. It is a good bet that putting medication into our bodies is unlikely to make us more fulfilled in life. There are some obvious exceptions like our depression or asthma medication. But the promise of ingesting something that brings with it a better life is the stuff of drug and alcohol addiction. The odds are also good that something that costs money is not likely to give us a fuller life. Once again there are some exceptions; your first home ownership or dental bills to give your child a better smile may be some of the exceptions. But in general we do not ingest a happier or fuller life, and we also do not purchase our life satisfaction and contentment. Although this is common sense when you think about it, product marketing in this country spends billions to convince you otherwise.

We do not improve our lives by working even harder than we do now to have more money to spend on the dwindling leisure time we are left with. We do not add to our life by spending more time on pursuits that take us away from family and friends to have more economic resources to provide for our family. In fact most any thoughts that money is going to significantly add to our satisfaction in life are likely to be pipe dreams. Repeated studies have indicated that after we lift ourselves out of poverty, additional financial resources do little to add to our happiness.

Pick up any travel magazine or book, and you will see that happiness awaits you if only you travel to the location in the spotlight. But wait, that beautiful place in the picture is right down the road that I pass all the time and don't even notice. Those of us who travel more than we would like to, know that in the Washington D.C. airport are posters to go see the Rockies in Colorado, and in the Denver airport are posters to go to Washington D.C. It would seem that the world of travel is all about selling you on the "grass is greener" approach to living. It has always been clear to me that I don't need to travel anywhere to be happy or to be miserable, I can do both right where I find myself.

Baker and Stauth have some other thoughts on what to do and not do to achieve happiness and personal contentment (Baker & Stauth, 2002):

1. You can't buy happiness, so save your money.
2. Pleasure is fine, but it is the dessert of life and not the meal.
3. You can spend your life savings on therapy trying to resolve past traumas; strive instead to transcend the past (so they agree with the premise of this book).
4. Few of us actually overcome all our weaknesses, so put your focus in maximizing your strengths.
5. You can't force happiness just as you can't plan spontaneity. Happiness is a combination of many factors and you can't just decide some afternoon to be a happy person from now on.

So if gratifying yourself, spending money, working harder, and getting away from it all are poor strategies to a more fulfilled life, then what does science tell us that actually works? I am glad you asked. I will answer this question with some ideas from positive psychology (Boehm & Lyubomirsky, in press) and a few of my own.

Fifteen Straightforward Action Steps to Life Satisfaction

Individually or in groups, these action steps can give you an excellent return on your investment. They are not presented in any particular order of importance:

1. Believe in yourself - be on your side.

I work with many traumatized people, both adults and children. It is not a compliment when someone says to you, "Stop being defensive." However, I have learned that there are times when being defensive is a definite positive. Many traumatized people do not subject themselves to scrutiny and do not put ideas out because they believe they will likely be shot down by smarter, wiser, or at least more forceful individuals. Defending one's ideas and positions is a critical ability of someone who has learned self-confidence. I began to see the ability to defend oneself and one's ideas as a measure of health and of personal strength. There is no question that this asset of being defensive can go too far, but who will come to your defense and be on your side if you are not there for yourself?

2. Take an inventory of the adversity you have overcome.

A principle in solution-focused therapy is to help individuals consider how they have faced problems in the past similar to what they are facing today. The focus is on successful efforts, which we all have if we take the time to consider them. We all have the habit of believing that the worst problems are our own, and the most serious problems are the ones we are facing today. However, when we consider how we have faced adversity in the past we quickly see that we have faced conflicts and difficulties every bit as difficult as today's struggles, and many times the challenges of the past have been harder. You don't need to go through life with a score card, but it is helpful to consider all that you have come through, and how you are still going strong all these challenges later. Give yourself credit for your endurance and your hard work. The odds are that these two ingredients are exactly what your current problems will demand from you to be successful.

3. Develop a positive outlook.

There is just no substitute for a positive outlook. We need to remember that we create the world we live in and we do so in many ways. The most important way we create our world is in the way we choose to think and feel about what goes on in our lives. We will always have the choice of seeing the negatives in a good day, or seeing the positives in a terrible day. It is not just that we occupy our mind with negative thoughts or feelings. Our body follows the lead of our brain in producing a cascade of internal reactions that either stress the body or bring about calm. A positive disposition will allow you to view the world as a more hospitable place, live in a more manageable environment, feel better about yourself and others, prompt your body to heal faster and avoid illness, encourage more natural highs or peak experiences, and improve your support system. Having a positive and optimistic outlook is the single most important step anyone can take to bring about improvement in all aspects of our lives.

4. Forgive others.

Forgiveness is a cornerstone of many religions. Starting early as children we are taught to forgive others. What is not emphasized enough, but should be, is to stress forgiveness of self. As with love, I do not believe we can forgive others without being able to forgive ourselves. So it is important to start at home and forgive yourself for being flawed, for making mistakes, for stupid decisions, and for all the times you had an opportunity in life and ended up throwing it away or making a mess of things. We all do it, we all are guilty, and we all pay the built-in price for our flaws, so why not try some forgiveness.

Although forgiveness is a cornerstone of religious beliefs, it can be a much trickier issue in psychology when it comes to traumatized individuals. If you want to raise the temperature in a room some time just tell a group of trauma survivors, or for that matter a group of trauma therapists, that it is a good idea to forgive your abuser. We know that spiritually this is sound theology; for example Christians ask God to forgive them as they forgive others in the Lord's prayer. But forgive an abuser, an offender, let someone off the hook for violating you and bringing so much pain and sadness into your life?[2] The quick answer is "yes," but it is strong medicine and takes great strength. The most powerful thing you can do is to forgive someone who has harmed you. You may have every right to be angry, to blame, and to seek retribution. But none of these things frees you from the harm done to you. The more you have to forgive, the more you get back if you can walk this steep slope. Forgiveness is life affirming, it is compassionate, it is loving the forgiven person, and it is, most of all, empowering and affirming of yourself. It is Ghandi in the lice-filled uniform in prison telling the guards, "Thank you for this chance to learn to forgive," and really meaning it. It

---

2. *This is a complex issue when considering the elements of healing abuse, including being clear on who is responsible. But we need to move beyond responsibility in order to work to be free of the abuse.*

is Jesus on the cross choosing to end his life with forgiving his accusers and his executioners. Now that is the power that can only come from love.

5. Be thankful every day.

Each year I make a big deal of Thanksgiving to the children I live and work with. To me this day is not a celebration of gluttony that comes once a year. I tell the children it is a reminder that being thankful is important one full day a year, and small parts of every other day throughout the year. When we stop and think about what we have, how can we not experience some level of thanks? Being thankful is not time consuming, it is not expensive, and it is certainly not painful in any way. So why not build it into each day in some form? I start every day with a few quiet moments of thanks, and I end every day in the same way. For me the challenge starting and ending the day is not hard because it is my routine. The hard part is to be thankful for the joys as well as the hardships that come our way. This may sound like some syrupy platitude, but it is not. When we are thankful for our challenges and our difficulties, we gain more power over problems in our life. When we are thankful for the bad times, the good times turn out to be even better. Give it a try and see for yourself.

6. Ask for what you need from others.

What is so difficult about asking for what you need? Nothing, but few of us are good at it. Some of us expect our needs to be met without asking. Somehow it doesn't mean so much if we have to ask. For others we don't want to put someone out by asking for time or attention. After all, the other people have their own needs and issues, they don't want mine as well. Still other people do not want to be vulnerable, or create expectations that the favor must be returned. My grandmother, who lived most of her life in Oklahoma, would call that "being beholden" and that was a bad thing for independent-minded people. These and many other reasons keep us from reaching out to others. Yet we all need each other throughout our lives, even if we pretend we do not. Try something new if you are one of these people and learn to ask for what you need from others. Start small with little things and build up to more important things as you get better at it. The better you are at asking for what you need and want, the happier you will become. Sounds worth it to me, what do you think?

7. Structure time each day to be alone and quiet, and use this time for reflection.

Quiet time each day has many names. Many years ago it was called a morning constitutional. It also goes by a solitary walk, meditation, prayer, contemplation, and spiritual practice. Regardless of the name it goes by, the process is usually the same. Remove yourself from the stresses of daily life, relax, breathe deeply and settle your mind, body and spirit. Some people have a routine that they involve themselves in to recharge their batteries, to think through a problem situation, or even to be more productive the rest of the day. On a spiritual level being alone and quiet is generally done for the purpose of going deeper into oneself or communing with God or your higher power. Regardless of the way you do this or why you do this, it is a very good idea to build in the time to make this happen in your day. It does not take much time, and the rewards are great as long as you are looking for clarity, presence and calm. These types of calm, quiet time also help you to develop an awareness of what is going on around you and how you fit in. This could be called developing the internal witness to your world. This means having the presence to observe what is around you and to be aware of the choices you are making at any time. It also means that you have the ability to step outside of yourself and watch yourself. Many people go through life on auto pilot. They see events that go on in their lives as random and out of their control. Being a witness to your own life and exercising control over the things you can manage is what this book is all about. A reminder each day to live in this way is highly recommended.

8. Take care of your body.

It would seem logical that everyone should take care of their body, but this simply is not the case. There are many ways that we mistreat ourselves each and every day. It may be in what we eat, what we wear, what we do or what we don't do. For example, it simply makes no sense how many people do not get health-producing exercise. Some people work too much, and others don't put in effort to produce the result of making their bodies work. Some individuals smoke, others drink to excess or engage in risky or unhealthy behavior such as taking drugs to excess. There is no limit to the ways that people abuse their bodies. Some people neglect their bodies. It is not what they do but what they don't do that discourages health.

9. Plan something in your near future that will recharge your batteries.

It may seem a trivial practice, but I help myself get through difficult times by planning a reward at the end. I do this in small and large ways. If I must write a report that I am not looking forward to, I treat myself when I am finished with a break or something I am looking forward to. I hold off on some tasks of living that have little enjoyment until right before I am to do something I like. Just before a game of golf, for example, is a great time to clean the bathroom. But this strategy is not just effective when you are facing a difficult or tedious activity. Look to the future and plan something that you would love to do, but that will take planning in advance to make it happen. You might be surprised how many friends you can get together for a one-of-a-kind event—you don't have to wait until the next Super Bowl for an excuse for a party. Whether plans for fun are big or small, there is plenty of stress and difficulties coming your way that will take your energy. Do your best to plan something to recharge and put an investment of energy back into your account.

10. Spend time and energy with family.

Let me first say that by family I mean the people you most care about in life. This may be a spouse, parents, children, and relatives, but it could also mean the intentional family that provides you with support in life such as friends and companions. The strength of birth families is that we are stuck with our connections, so no matter how much my brother may want to dissolve our brotherhood, he can't. This gives us some breathing room in our relationship. We may want to run away from our connection, but we remain brothers. This is not the case with friends, lovers, or even the modern marriage. It is just the nature of these chosen connections that make them so special. I did not pick my relatives, and I may have chosen someone else for the role had I a choice. But I did pick my spouse, my friends and the people I chose to spend my time with. I think it was Kahlil Gibran who said, "For what is your friend that you should seek him with hours to kill? Seek him always with hours to live."

Invest in your family and your friends if you want a good return. For that matter, particularly invest in your birth family, if you can manage to be under the same roof without violence. A number of years ago I realized my brothers (I was not blessed with a sister) and parents seldom traveled from the distances we all lived to be together. I took the initiative and asked if they were interested in getting together on a yearly basis. The response was, "sure." It just took someone to ask. We have had many laughs as well as some struggles in our annual get-togethers. Give more to those you love, and you are likely to get more in return.

11. Send someone a letter letting them know you value them being in your life.

People expect cards on their birthday, and I will guarantee you that my mother expects to hear from me on Mother's Day, as well she should after all she has done for me. Special occasions are actually not the best times to let someone know how much they mean to you. A birthday card is great, but would not have been sent if the calendar said it was a different day. Sit down and write a letter to someone when there is no reason to do so other than the message you are sending. You could go see the person and tell them how you feel in person. This approach is fine, but is more difficult and may not have as much impact.

I suggest writing for several reasons. First, you get a chance to communicate your message just the way you want to—no interruptions and no immediate responses. You can write it, put it down and read it again later to see if it is just what you want to say. The second reason is that the other person will read a letter, but for a variety of reasons may not hear all you say verbally. Third, the person has your message that can be reread later, and the reader will not be able to change what he thinks you said and remember only what he chooses to remember.

Surprise someone with a letter that lays out your message. Recently I did this with a friend and received an immediate call inquiring whether I was dying and putting my affairs in order. This was a sign to me that such a communication from me was overdue if the other person would only expect it if I had been given only a few weeks to live. Don't do it for this reason. You will likely increase the chances that you will receive a letter in return, hopefully a positive one!

12. Develop coping strategies for stress.

Stress is one thing in life that we cannot avoid. We may have some choice in the type and volume of stress, but no one gets out of life alive, and this reality is sufficient for stress throughout life. The important thing to being fulfilled in life is to manage the stress that you have. Your attitude is critically important when it comes to stress management. I like to use the analogy of whitewater river rafting. Two people in the same raft can go through the same event and have completely different experiences. One can scream with delight while the cold water hits her face, while someone else two feet away screams with terror and just knows his end will come in this cold, unfriendly water. What is the difference between a great time and a frightening experience? The person's attitude is the difference, and we all determine our experience based upon how we perceive our situation and our ability to impact what we are doing.

ॐॐ

Choose your own adventure

My wife loves thrill rides in amusement parks, but hates experiences such as rock climbing or other activities with what she calls real danger. I, on the other hand, have done technical mountain climbing including a 1,500 foot vertical spire in Arizona, and for me there is nothing more frightening than a roller coaster. I know why some people like them: it is a controlled and exciting experience from which they know they will walk away. For me the visceral experience of such "entertainment" rides is the same as what many people have for their last experience of life — hurtling through space with no steering wheel and no brake on your way to certain death. OK, so control is an issue for me. The stress of a thrill ride is real or people wouldn't pay money to do it. It is one of those stresses in life that I have no interest in managing, so Joyce rides and I watch, and we both choose our own adventure. Each and every day we all choose our own adventure.

Unlike amusement rides, we don't stand in line and choose some of our stresses in life. Bad things happen to good people, and the older and wiser I become, the more I see that security is a myth in life. When a person believes that he has achieved control over things, his control may end with a drunk driver, his next medical check-up, or an unexpected stroke, among other things. Stress is a fact of life, and the more we experience stress, the better we are able to learn how to cope with stress. But there is a challenge to learning from stress rather than being overwhelmed by it. The challenge is that we must not let stress get the upper hand, although nearly every stress signals the brain that it is bigger than our ability to handle it.

We all have ways to manage stress that may or not work or may or may not be healthy. I was recently asked what the difference between adapting to stress and coping with stress. My answer was that we all adapt to stress, but adaptation may not be positive or healthy. A depressed individual may adapt to a stressful life with continual drug consumption, both legal and illegal. But coping indicates a successful adaptation and a healthy way to face the challenges of living. There are many ways to build healthy coping into our daily lives. Here are just a few: running or aerobic exercise, meditation, biking, Tai Chi, athletics and team sports, Yoga, reading, music, the expressive arts, acting, gardening, walking alone or with a pet, hobbies, study and personal advancement, time with a friend, prayer and spiritual practice, yard work, horseback riding, camping and hiking, mountain climbing, flying, swimming and diving, knitting, breathing exercises, shopping, working on your car, cleaning, playing with a child, volunteering time to help someone else, going to the theatre or seeing a good movie, writing, sightseeing, watching sunsets, having a solitary walk on the beach, driving, woodworking, and an endless number of activities available to all of us. Only when we develop new thoughts and new neuropathways related to stress do we begin to get the upper hand and cope with stress rather than be controlled by it.

13. Expand your support system and increase time with our support system.

For all the reasons that have been addressed, it should be very clear at this point that support is a critical component of surviving and thriving in life. We start out needing the support of others to live; we rely on the support of a family to protect us, care for our needs and teach us what we need to know in life. As teens we switch our interest from our family to our chosen family of peers. As adults we create our own family with a partner and perhaps children, but also an intentional family of friends and people we spend our work time with and others we spend our free time with. One of the best ways to enhance our satisfaction with our life is to take specific steps to expand our support network. Some people do this quickly by joining a club or joining a faith community. Others do this by being more social and extending invitations to others and accepting invitations in return. There are many ways to involve more people in our life who we want to be there. It would not enhance your life to join the local chapter of the Hell's Angels if you don't like motorcycles or get nervous around leather-clad, tattooed, and somewhat scary looking bikers. It is not just that we increase our social contacts, we have to invite the right people into our life. When men or women are incarcerated, there are social networks that develop, but not necessarily ones that would have developed on the "outside." We need like-minded individuals who have similar interests to our own.

Once we increase the size of our social support system, then it is a very good idea to increase the amount of time we invest in this network. People tend to respond when you give the signals that you are interested in them. Spending time with a friend or a group of friends is an important statement of interest in others and will often result in this interest being returned to you. One exercise you can do is to make a list of people you can go to and share a problem with. If your list is long, you will likely have more life satisfaction than if your list is significantly shorter. Although it is fine to invest heavily in one or two "best friends," support systems are one place where the more there are, the merrier.

14. Help someone.

A guaranteed way to get out of yourself and your own problems, at least for a while, is to reach out and help someone. This can come in the many forms. Volunteering is a coordinated activity in most medium to larger communities around the country. You can feed the homeless, help out at your child's school, read to the blind, help out at the local domestic violence shelter, or be a big sister for a child who needs an older and wiser friend. You can't give the type of energy to others that you think is valuable if you are obsessed with yourself or your problems. We must extricate ourselves from ourselves, and then we can be with another person. When this happens we do a number of important things that change our perspective in life. We get more perspective when we see that others have their own problems, many times more difficult that what we struggle with. We "walk a mile in someone else's moccasins" and learn to empathize and develop more compassion. We also engage in the great paradox of helping, that the more you give, the more you receive. Many years ago I volunteered to be a Hospice volunteer and helped people through the dying process. As challenging as this was at times, I never questioned for a second that I was getting much more back than I was giving. I say this even though the people I had the great fortune to be with were in their final months, weeks and days. To a person, these people were very thankful for every moment I gave them. It was a time in my life that I experienced unconditional love, walking into a room and seeing the dying person light up because I was there once again. I may have been a volunteer, but I was paid in love, meaning, and purpose more than with any other activity I have ever done in my life.

15. Join a community based on spiritual beliefs.

One way that many people put most of these steps into practical application is to join a support system of people who help each other and have beliefs and values such as forgiveness, love, and compassion. They find a group of people who are thankful for what they have been given, and they get together to celebrate their blessings and in the process fill their lives with more meaning and purpose. Now this may not describe every church or faith community in the country, but it is the goal of every spiritual community. You may need to visit several such groups before finding the right one, but they exist and are a great help and support to those fortunate enough to find such a spiritual home.

Don't dismiss this step by saying, "Who wants to sit in the back of a large church and listen to bad organ music and then try to get out of the parking lot quickly to avoid missing part of the ball game?" Large churches with organ music may or may not be on your list. But there are many other types of spiritual communities that don't include an organ and have nothing to do with a church. Most of the people in the United States believe in God, and the majority are affiliated with a religion. If this is what you consider a spiritual community, then great; if not, don't discard this method of building life satisfaction unless you consider the many types of communities that exist around what you do believe.

As a therapist all of my adult life, I often hear adults say that they no longer believe what they were taught as children. However, many stop with this statement and have never taken the next step to determine for themselves what they do believe. Unless we do this, we will not find the fullest life satisfaction that could be available, and we will not find others who have come up with the same answer we have and support each other along the path of life.

What Must I Do to Be Happy, to Be Satisfied, and to Find Personal Contentment?

There have been many answers to the question "what must I do to be happy and satisfied and to find personal contentment?" addressed in the previous chapters. For many people on the planet, life is a challenge simply to survive. This may be due to living in a war zone, being the member of the wrong ethnic group during genocide or ethnic cleansing, or simply trying to find enough to eat each day to be able to see another sunrise. There are many other people who find the challenges of life too difficult to bear without relying on ways to make the pain go away in one form or another. We have whole industries providing legal and illegal drugs, alcohol, sex for hire, and fantasy for sale that promises to take us away from our lives of toil, if only for a short while.

As a marriage counselor I note with dismay that over 50 percent of marriages end in divorce in America. My observation is that another 25 percent stay together unhappily because economics, children, family pressure or simply habit prevent a divorce. Of the remaining 25 percent of married people, 10 percent tell themselves they are happy but don't like to think about it too much, or upon reflection they might change their minds. There are another 10 percent who feel satisfied with what they have with their partner. Finally, this leaves approximately 5 percent of married people who live in a dynamic, fulfilling relationship of living truth. These people look forward to seeing each other at the end of the day, not to avoid loneliness and have someone to be with, but to see someone to bring their joy, their pain, their excitement, and their flaws. Someone who simultaneously supports, loves and pushes self and partner to fulfill their potential in all respects of their lives. The above observations are not scientific, or based on research. In fact, social research would reflect a more positive picture than the above. But I stand by my anecdotal observations because there are many people who self-report a better marriage and a better life than they have. They do this in order to avoid facing the truth or in an attempt to convince themselves they have it better than they do.

I bring this up because a similar observation could be made about life in general. Although human beings may be preset to be happy, most of us fall short of this goal. Of the many reasons for this, one of the most frequent is because something very bad has robbed the individual of the hope or even the desire to strive to be happy, fulfilled, and content. Philosophers, authors and teachers have always tried to identify the keys to happiness, and I am a very minor example in a long list of purveyors of hope. But hearing about, reading about, and watching the movie about a mountain is not the same as climbing it and finding out for yourself both the struggles and the exhilaration of the journey. I am writing to myself as much as I am to you, and quite frankly I would like to have more company on the trail up the mountain. So before this book concludes, I want to make one more attempt to go right at this question of what I must do to find personal contentment.

Happiness takes time to master, but is well worth the effort. Skills needed for happiness as well as self-confidence, satisfaction, and personal contentment are gradually learned and can develop into a positive cycle of success. It is through these positive skills that we achieve some of the important qualities that we all desire and that lead to personal contentment: love, optimism, courage, freedom, personal initiative, security, health, spirituality, altruism, perspective, humor and purpose (Baker & Stauth, 2002).

Martin Seligman in his writings identifies three ways to promote the journey to a full and satisfying life that were mentioned earlier (Seligman, 1998; Seligman, 2002). These are:

1. Get more pleasure and enjoyment out of what you do.
2. Become more engaged in your activities and your life.
3. Find ways to make your life more meaningful by finding purpose.

Increasing the Pleasure and Enjoyment in Your Life

The first way to achieve more enjoyment is through increasing the amount of pleasure you experience. Many of us have been raised in a post-puritanical moral climate in which pleasure is somehow suspect. If this was not the case we would not have needed a sexual revolution in the 60's or the "greed is good" mentality of the 80's. Many of us were brought up to believe that if it feels good, it must be illegal, immoral, or both. If a child rubs his sore arm because it feels good that is one thing, if he rubs his penis that is something entirely different. But sex is only one form of pleasure we have been warned against. For most pleasures there is a corresponding cardinal sin. For leisure we must beware of sloth, for the transcendent experience of sexual union we walk a fine line with lust, for the love of food there is gluttony waiting to pervert us, and so on. Pleasure has often been given a bad name by cultural mores and religions for less than helpful reasons.

Pleasure should not be avoided and is essential in living. The pleasure principle is fundamental to our learning safe and satisfying behaviors as children. We instinctively pursue what is pleasurable and avoid what is painful. If we did not, we could have very short and miserable lives indeed, as many people do. We must move as individuals and as a society away from being either suspicious of pleasure or holding pleasure as our only goal. Human beings have found creative ways to pervert everything that is good and wholesome. Loving sexual ecstasy is not the same as prurient lust; however I believe there is more than a little eros and lust in healthy sexual lovemaking. The same could be said for the pleasure of food, of leisure, of sensuality and of everything that in fact brings us enjoyment and pleasure.

There are some people who do not avoid pleasure, who in fact attempt to build a life around it. This takes financial resources in order to maximize the ability to build the ultimately pleasurable life. One of many examples could be the life of Hugh Hefner. As a psychologist I have been fascinated by this man and his philosophy for many years. I am interested in anything that can help result in a full and happy life. Hefner may be one of the best examples of someone who has pursued happiness by maximizing pleasure of any and every type. He may be the most persistent icon of the sexual revolution. But it is not only the pleasure of sexuality that he pursues and advocates. He is the preacher of all that is pleasurable from food to leisure, fine possessions, fast times, ultimate parties, literature, entertainment, power and influence, celebrity, and, yes, sex. He appears to have done pretty well living the way he has, at least that is what it looks like from the outside. As he moves into his 80s it will be fascinating to see if the pleasures of the world continue to hold the same importance and provide the same return as they did in his younger years.

Consistent pleasure may actually be neurologically impossible due to the saturation of neuro-transmitters that then block the release of serotonin and dopamine. It is a good idea to take a break from a personal pleasure in order to come back and enjoy it again (did you hear that Mr. Hefner?). As the old country song goes, "After you've been having steak for a long time, beans, beans taste fine." I like Dan Baker's statement, "Pleasure is a good thing, but remember it is the dessert of life and not the meal" (Baker & Stauth, 2002).

True pleasure is a good thing and we should work to bring more of it into our lives. It is a far cry better than pain, and if we keep pleasure in balance and do not pervert it, it leads to enjoyment, which in turn lifts our spirits, lightens our heavy load, and helps recharge our battery for more of life's heavy lifting. It is healthy to have things in your life that make you feel good and that make you happy at least for a while. Temporary happiness is limited but is better than temporary depression. Many things bring us pleasure: hobbies, interests, food, sunsets, and snowflakes that land on our nose and eyelashes. Pleasure is a wonderful part of living, and it is a natural drive when to pursue pleasure and avoid pain. However, pleasure is always fleeting and temporary.

Become More Engaged in What You Do

To move to a more substantial level of satisfaction we must become more engaged in living. This includes being engaged with people, with beliefs, with activities, with work, with loved ones, and with everything around us that we care about. Back to the Hospice work I mentioned earlier, there were few partners who, after losing a loved one, did not say something like, "I would give anything to have just one more day with him/her before the illness." But there were days before the illness, many of them. When we engage in what we have that brings us joy, energy, or excitement, we fill our lives with satisfaction that goes beyond temporary pleasure.

As enjoyable as pleasure can be, it has its limits. Perhaps the main limit of pleasure is that it is transitory. Because pleasure is primarily associated with the senses, it must change. Beautiful sunsets have a habit of setting, when you drink your favorite wine it is gone, and when all of your friends come to your birthday bash and have a great time, the next day it is back to work and no longer is everyone going out of their way to treat you in a special way. Some philosophers have pointed out that pleasure has a depressing side to it in that if one goes up, one must come down. The Stoics of centuries ago warned against the highs and lows of pleasure, and Buddha pointed out that craving or attachment to pleasure was actually the root of all suffering. Buddha observed that if we embraced everything that comes our way in life, including dying, we would eliminate the attachment or suffering that comes with wanting something other than what we have.

Since pleasure has limits on how much happiness and personal contentment it can offer us, how can we go beyond these limits? One answer is to build more engagement with people, places and experiences into our lives. We have all had the experience of an activity going on around us where we have the choice of getting involved or sitting this one out. Engagement allows us to invest more, to connect more and to put more time, energy, and personal significance into the situation. In turn this allows for more of a return on our investment.

I remember going to dances in school. I don't think I am alone when I say these were some of the most difficult times for me growing up socially. It was so difficult to walk across the dance floor (the boys invariably were on one side and the girls on the other) and ask a girl to dance. I remember waiting dance after dance to get up the courage to ask a girl only to be ready and watch her leave with someone else, or tap a girl and the shoulder and see that someone was on the other side of her and had asked first. Of course the worst was the polite, "No, thank you." I can recall that it was always polite and never, "Dance with you? Yuck!" But even the polite rejections meant the walk back to the other side of the room alone and your "friends" seizing this opportunity to rub it in. But it was just these difficult times of life that helped each of us learn and find out about ourselves. Much more than the rejections, I remember the times the girl said yes with a smile. I remember the frightening phone calls to ask her out on a date, and when the answer was yes, there was nothing like such a time as a teen.

I was secretly trying to decide whether to ask out a wonderful, smart and friendly girl in my senior class in high school named Joyce. At a gathering of my buddies, a friend announced that he had decided to ask this beautiful girl named Joyce to the big dance coming up. I quickly announced that he was too late because she was going with me. He was angry that I had "aced him out," and another friend said, "you snooze and you lose, Dan." I didn't exactly lie when I implied that she was going to the dance with me, but the truth was I had not asked her yet. As soon as my friends left, I called, she said yes, and we have been a couple since that big dance 41 years ago. In fact as I wrote the above she came into my office, I read this to her, and she had tears in her eyes, as did I.

If we sit out the dance, we protect ourselves from rejection, but we prevent ourselves from engagement. The carnival barkers have it right when they say, "If you don't play, you can't win." Carrying my school dance example one step further, Lee Ann Womack has a song that addresses engagement in life, *I Hope You Dance*. But what about what Buddha said, shouldn't you avoid being attached to having fun at the dance or you will suffer? Perhaps this is one interpretation but I prefer to think of Buddha dancing, but without being attached to doing so with a particular person and therefore not able to be rejected. He never said not to live; he did say to live mindfully and with compassion for all living things.

Long after the big dance my senior year in high school, I found myself a therapist for ten years in Phoenix working with children and their families. It was very fulfilling work in a city that was often hot, but an enjoyable environment to live in. I had no major complaints with this life, but it seemed there must be more and I needed to find what more I could do with my most productive professional and personal years of life. A journey of considering many factors and many possibilities ended up with our own Oregon Trail to a place where we knew no one, a place we had never been. Here we would find a new way to engage more fully in life, to integrate our personal and professional lives, and to perform works of service beyond what we had ever done before. The result of this journey was all this and more, and has resulted in the story of Jasper Mountain (*www.jaspermountain.org*). This story reaches a milestone in 2007 with the 25th anniversary of this experience of near total engagement in life, in service to others, and in changing our lives for the better while changing the lives of others.

With the unique work of Jasper Mountain over the last 25 years, I have made many friends and, surprising to me, many enemies. We miserably failed in our efforts to keep our work quiet and get no publicity. As the publicity grew from local to regional to national and international, people either viewed our work as wonderful or terrible, and very few people seem undecided. You may ask how anyone could view people with mistrust who are giving their professional careers, their money and resources, and their very lives to live with violent, emotionally disturbed children who had been so badly abused that they learned to abuse others.

I cannot tell you why, but I can confirm that there are many people who have their own reasons to see me and my organization as problematic and even misguided. During the writing of this book we experienced the most turbulent times of our organization's history with individuals, attorneys, and regulatory organizations pressuring us to change our belief that we can truly help children change their lives from within, much the same as the message of this book. What is wrong with this belief? Some call it naive, some say it is out of step with current thinking, and some (bureaucrats) claim it is too expensive. What frustrates and actually makes it worse for all our critics is our documented success rates with children that families and other professionals and programs called unworkable. The story of Jasper Mountain is a story of total engagement. It is a story of great highs and lows, a story of how I have received more personal contentment than I could ever have imagined sitting comfortably in the Phoenix sun 25 years ago, as I now sit watching the rain in Oregon.

One poignant image for me is the Christian Bible story of the rich man putting a large sum of money into the temple basket and saying a prayer out loud of thanks to

God. He was followed by the poor woman who quietly put one copper coin in the basket and prayed silently to herself. Jesus explained who received the greatest return and reward on the investment. It was not the rich man with the large amount of money, it was the poor woman because "she gave everything she had." Total engagement in life is what can produce maximum return.

It is not just winning and losing, or getting the girl if you are a teenager. Engagement is about putting something of yourself into whatever you are dealing with: your job, your school, your friends, your children, your spouse, your spiritual faith, and the next hour of your life. Will you dance or will you sit this one out? Engagement raises the bar in life. It infuses anything you do with extra importance and enhances meaning, which is our next step on the path to personal contentment.

Find Purpose in Your Activities and More Meaning in Your Life

Much like pleasure, engagement can also have its limits in providing happiness and personal contentment. There are many examples of famous leaders in history who enjoyed the finer and more pleasurable things of life, and were very engaged pursuing their interests. But some of these individuals are the antithesis of a fulfilled, happy or content person. The Roman emperor Diocletian comes to mind. He filled every waking moment with wine, women (and boys) and song, with an occasional break to run the empire. The excessive pursuit of pleasure and gratification of the Roman emperors is legendary and, from my study and trips to Rome, apparently quite historically factual. Like Diocletian, many other emperors had unlimited resources, held total power and control, and essentially wrote the rules as they went along (the dream of every dictator throughout history as well as our own time). They were engaged in a life of power, lust, and revenge including unspeakable spectacles of mass crucifixions and feeding enemies to lions. But were they happy or content? Not from our best reading of history. The limits of pleasure and engagement include the need to find purpose and meaning in the things in which we are engaged (other than keeping control of the world by paying off supporters and killing your enemies).

We certainly do not have to go back millennia to see that pleasure and engagement are not enough. I previously made reference to Bill Gates, whom other software moguls might consider a modern corporate emperor (I'm quite sure he would take exception to such a comparison). He has been the richest man in the world twelve years in a row now with unlimited resources to pursue pleasure. He also is famously engaged in his life and his business, but something apparently was lacking. Bill clearly is both smart and wise. To fix this lack, he left his ideal job and began the pursuit of bringing meaning and purpose to his efforts, his wealth, and his life.

The top of the happiness and personal contentment ladder is meaning and purpose. In fact, it is very possible to skip the pleasure part and go straight to meaning and purpose, although this is not easy and not necessarily recommended. An example is Mother Teresa. She had little interest or willingness to be involved in pleasurable pursuits (something she shared with Gandhi, Francis of Assisi, the Desert Fathers, and the Dalai Lama), but this small frail nun had unlimited energy coming from her purpose to rid the world of hunger and loneliness. Mother Teresa not only did not ask for corporate dollars to help the poor, she would not accept them. Instead she asked those who wished to give resources to her to instead give these resources directly and personally to the poor themselves. She understood that in her short lifetime hunger would not be eliminated (even Jesus said, "The poor will always be with you)." But she understood better that it is not only the dream but the journey that is important to finding your spiritual purpose and your highest attainment of personal contentment.

There is a risk with my using such examples. The risk is that we ordinary people will see our weakness and limitations and say we are no Gandhi and no Mother Teresa. Using these examples of famously engaged people pursuing meaning and purpose of the highest order leaves us with too great a distance between who we see in the mirror and what we read of these great souls (Mahatma was not Gandhi's first name, it was a title meaning "great soul"). Using these great people is easier for me than using myself, but a few pages back I shared that my own path in engaging a higher purpose than myself by helping abused children has brought me much more than I have ever invested, and I say this at a time in which my life has never had so much conflict. I want serenity in my life, but more than this I want to have a reason to get up each morning and fully engage in the world I have created and the activities I choose. I wouldn't mind some pleasure along the way, but much more I want to live my life for a purpose to serve the greater good, in my case to give children who are coming from lives of violence, isolation, and misery a chance at success.

Every one of the examples of famous people I have cited value people with great flaws and limitations. I assure you that I also have great flaws and limitations (just ask my wife Joyce, yes the one from the senior dance). The great equalizer of flaws and limitations is a desire and commitment to pursue meaning and purpose in life. There are no limits to making a difference on the planet. One of my personal dilemmas is that while I am engaged in the meaning and purpose I have found, I see so many other important efforts I could be making with my time and talents. It is one of my flaws that I must work to accept this fact.

Meaning and purpose do not require ending hunger on the planet, disarming all nuclear weapons, saving the whales, or wearing no fur or cosmetics where animals are harmed. Some people keep themselves from doing anything by saying to themselves that they can't possibly do enough that would make a difference. Such a position is not only incorrect, but it robs us of finding the key to the greatest level of happiness and personal contentment available to us. Margaret Mead is often quoted as saying, "Never doubt that a small group of committed citizens can change the world; indeed, it is the only thing that ever has."

⇛⇝

The path to personal contentment

Unfortunately, no one finds the love of his or her life and lives happily ever after. Few people fulfill their dreams. We can never succeed in life unless we risk failure. Personal contentment is not the absence of stress or of failure, it is a state of being in which all that one experiences is put into perspective and is the object of consideration and growth. Satisfaction is not the absence of bad times, but a belief in the ability to turn even bad times into something that is good. A full life is not taking up space on the planet trying to avoid problems, it is taking on problems head on with confidence and optimism. Personal contentment and happiness are not the absence of anything, particularly anything bad, they are the presence of awareness of all that is involved in living, breathing, hurting, and loving. Personal contentment is the result of a life truly lived, and bringing to all of life the influence available to us to impact our experience and our world. Personal contentment will not make you monetarily wealthy or famous, but it will enrich your days with the birthright available to us all. We have all been given the ability to create our own experience and our own way in life that is nothing short of a divine gift. We can use such a gift to change ourself and thereby change the world. Or we can squander the gift with a life that too often is a glass half empty. Do not let the bad things in life lessen the wonder and value of the good things. It is your choice, and it is my choice.

෩෩

Engagement is great and adds a great deal to our lives, but if we want it all, we have to move to the top of the life satisfaction ladder, which is meaning and purpose. It is hard to separate the concepts of meaning and purpose. They form parts of a singular state of being. We find meaning when our values and our beliefs are integrally linked with what we are doing. We find purpose when we experience the importance and value of what we do. Meaning and purpose are the top of the career satisfaction ladder as well. It is great to be good at what you do, it is even better to be recognized by others as being great at what you do. However, it is best to be recognized for being good at something that changes the world for the better, or improves the lives of others. Finding meaning and purpose in life answers most of the core questions we all have. It helps us feel the greatest certainty we can feel in life. If what I am contemplating doing will have great meaning and will have an important purpose, the question becomes how do I do this, not should I do this.

Some of us are blessed with a profession and a job that have great meaning and purpose. I am one of those lucky people and I am constantly grateful for this precious gift. My job and my life are all about serving others, and in particular helping those who have been beaten down in life. I have been lucky to work with frightened people, with battered people, with sexually abused people, and to have a specific career focused on helping traumatized children. I frequently say that no one has the job satisfaction that I do, and I believe this. I could broaden that and say that I should be thankful every day for having the life satisfaction that I do. But I am under the same spell as many others, in that there are days that I don't take the time to appreciate and be thankful for what I have. When I do take even a short moment to consider the meaning and purpose I have in my life, I am back to being the wealthiest person on the planet (did you hear that Mr. Gates?).

The Personal Contentment Inventory

So you give yourself passing grades on some areas and need improvement in other areas. If you care to break this down to specific issues, then take a piece of paper to write down your scores and take the following test. Keep in mind that it does not make much sense to answer any way but honestly; I'll never know either way, but you will. If you develop a plan coming from parts of this book, you may want to record your score and take the test periodically to see if you are headed in the direction you want to go and at the pace you wish.

For each of the following 20 questions give yourself a score of:

2 - If you do this most of the time
1 - If you do this some of the time
0 - If this is seldom true for you

Personal Contentment Inventory			
Do you bounce back when things go badly?	0	1	2
Do you laugh multiple times each day?	0	1	2
Do you make healthy lifestyle choices and avoid unhealthy behaviors?	0	1	2
Do you get pleasure and enjoyment out of what you do?	0	1	2
Do you invest yourself in your work and non-work activities?	0	1	2
Do you generally have a positive outlook?	0	1	2
Do you believe in and support yourself?	0	1	2
Do you ask for what you need from others?	0	1	2
Do you allow others to support you?	0	1	2
Do you have a personal belief system?	0	1	2
Does your belief system sustain you when life is difficult?	0	1	2
Do you use positive coping styles with the stress in your life?	0	1	2
Are you generally optimistic about your life?	0	1	2
Are you often grateful for what you have?	0	1	2
Do you share your good times and bad times with your support system?	0	1	2
Are your emotions primarily positive?	0	1	2
Do you thank others for being helpful, and forgive others when they aren't?	0	1	2

Personal Contentment Inventory			
Do you go out of your way to perform acts of kindness?	0	1	2
Do you make sure you spend positive time with your family and others you love?	0	1	2
Do you find ways to make your life more meaningful?	0	1	2
Totals			

Results

Add up your scores and total them. Then compare your total score to the following:

0-10   Your personal contentment is poor. You are likely overwhelmed by your life. Get help!

11-20 Your personal contentment is fair. You likely struggle with stress and disappointment. Make a plan of improvement.

21-30 Your personal contentment is good. You hold your own in life and meet your goals. Don't stop here, reach higher.

31-40 Your personal contentment is excellent. You are likely happy, satisfied, and healthy. Keep up the good work!

If you took the Personal Contentment Inventory, what do you do with the results? It is unlikely that the results are a surprise to you. If you are a miserable person you are not likely to find out that you are really quite content and just didn't know it. It is more likely that your score confirmed what you have been thinking and feeling about your life. This is not to say that you did find that you are actually doing better than you might often feel. We all tend to understate the positive in our lives at times at our own peril. But now that you have some external feedback on your level of personal contentment, what is your next step? (The only reason to score the inventory is to assist you in taking the next step in reaching the contentment you desire.)

A very low score is obviously cause for concern. People with low scores often prefer to put the responsibility on external circumstances. "I am not very happy with my life at present, but I just lost my job, unfairly I might add. I now have financial worries, and the job market is anything but positive. Just as soon as I get on my feet I will be more content." While there may be some influence of external factors, true personal content is generally not fundamentally concerned with events outside of you. If you have a low score, it would be a good idea to get some help in the form of a "contentment check-up." After all, we go to the doctor for a physical check-up, why not for a psychological or contentment check up? Who you discuss this with is your choice—a rabbi, a good friend, or a professional. Regardless of who you speak to, your score indicates a need for you to make some immediate changes in your contentment profile. Wouldn't you see your financial advisor if your investments were not producing a return? It may be time for some adjustments to produce a greater return on your life investments.

A score of fair would indicate that you may be holding your own, but there is more for you to get out of life. You may want to go back and look at the specific questions in the inventory that produced lower scores. It may be a good idea to develop a plan to address some of these areas. Here is a tip—choose one at a time to work on. Like exercise, do not overdo it. Pick an issue, put some time and energy into it, and, when you are seeing some improvement, add another issue.

If your scores are high or even excellent, there is less

immediacy in determining what more you want to do and when. However, due to the fact that you already have high personal contentment, the odds are very good that you will not stop where you are, nor should you. Personal contentment can be somewhat like the stock market, it does not stay the same for any period of time. It goes up and down and at times can do so dramatically. At times in your life you may be feeling a high degree of personal contentment, but it may be heavily influenced by everything going well in your life. When the unexpected or possibly a tragic event happens, what may have felt like internal contentment was more an internal mirror of external success. So even if your present score is high, take a good look to see if you contentment is coming from within and not from without.

Regardless of your score on the Personal Contentment Inventory it is important to point out that we cannot get more happiness in life by worrying about how miserable we are. Similarly we cannot develop more contentment by becoming stressed about getting more satisfaction out of living. Research on stress indicates that we do not change or grow to significant degrees if we have either very low stress or very high stress. Both can incapacitate a person. We grow most in a situation where there is moderate stress that can lead to action on our part. We talked previously about taking an inventory of how you are doing in your life, and perhaps you can take a few moments at the end of reading this book to consider just how you are doing and what more you want out of life. I would just ask you to remember the premise of these pages as you do so: if you want more out of life, you have the ability inside of you to get it by relying on your personal support system to cheer you on.

Success Can Have a Price

Most people would choose to be successful rather than

the other alternative. Success is not only a personal accomplishment but it could be assumed that with success in any endeavor comes the support and perhaps recognition of others. However, this assumption can often be inaccurate. Your personal success may not be celebrated or even welcomed by others and sometimes the source of such negativity directed at your success may come as a surprise.

I have watched the dynamic of success producing negativity and even resentment for a number of years now. While as a psychologist I can professionally understand this, as a person it has never made sense to me. I have been blessed with more than my share of success in my life. The awareness of the less-than-positive-reactions of others to things going well for me has gradually grown to the point that I now expect it. This is why I felt it important to add this issue near the end of this book. It can be very disconcerting to work hard and accomplish a personal goal only to find that your success has made you a target of criticism or disdain. Some less-than-positive responses to your success can come in the form of covertly ignoring you or your accomplishment. It may take the form of sour grapes — what's the big deal, anyone could have done it. You may find that such reactions are shared with others who let you know what is being said behind your back.

Perhaps more difficult to understand and accept are individuals with overtly hostile reactions to the success of others. This can also take a variety of forms. I will mention some of the more blatant examples I have personally experienced. When my non-profit corporation began to have financial success, a "friend" reported me to state auditors as an embezzler. As I began to gain growing respect for my professional expertise, a colleague began a rumor that I was a charlatan with fake post-graduate degrees because I had never gone to graduate school. As our child treatment programs began having regional prominence, a fellow child treatment program said publicly that we were actually harming children. As I began to have a national reputation for my work with the most severe children, a website listed me inaccurately as a dangerous proponent of harmful therapies. Despite my very public work to prevent and treat child abuse, I have on multiple occasions been investigated as a child abuser due to professionals who have put in harassment report about me to investigators. I actually was told on one occasion that although there has never been any substance to any of the false reports, "We are taking it seriously because we believe that where there is smoke there must be fire."

I have developed several non-profit programs, most of which have done well. As these programs have grown in public awareness, essentially each time they have been attacked by the least likely source of criticism — similar non-profit programs. The only explanation that makes any logical sense is professional jealousy, competition for community funding, or professional disagreement as to the program model. Whatever the justification people have used for their actions, this dynamic has surprised and shocked supporters of my programs. However, as I said earlier, I am no longer shocked and have even come to expect such attempts to diminish the success that I have found.

I frequently am approached by others who have a dream to develop a program of some type, and they ask how I have gone about setting up successful projects. After answering their questions, I always bring up the issue of who will want them to fail in their efforts. They generally look at me and wonder if I have a formal paranoid diagnosis (I don't for the record), but I ask them to write down my words and get back to me later and tell me if I was wrong in what I said.

If success can create new problems, they are better than the problems that come from failure. Everyone not saluting your accomplishments is no reason to hold back. Jealousy, envy, anger, and resentment are their problems, not yours. Overall, the problems that come with success are well worth the price.

I am certainly not the first to point out the dynamic of covert and overt negativity the comes with success. In recent times it would be difficult to find a person who did more for others in as altruistic and selfless way as Mother Teresa. And yet wherever this true saintly person went she encountered criticism and people questioning her motives. I offer here Mother Teresa's take on this issue with her recommendation to all of us:

People are often unreasonable, illogical and self-centered.
Forgive them anyway.
If you are kind, people may accuse you of selfish, ulterior motives.
Be kind anyway.
If you are successful, you will win some false friends and true enemies.
Succeed anyway.
If you are honest and frank, people may cheat you.
Be honest and frank anyway.
What you spend years building, someone could destroy overnight.
Build anyway.
If you find serenity and happiness, others may be jealous.
Be happy anyway.
The good you do today, people will forget tomorrow.
Do good anyway.
Give the world the best you have and it may never be good enough.
Give the world the best you have anyway.
You see, in the final analysis it is between you and God.
It was never between you and "them" anyway.

As wise and inspiring as these words are, we need to ask why a nun who inspired the world, was awarded the Nobel Peace Prize and will soon be a canonized Saint, would be able to write this. The answer is that she had these experiences over and over in her life. So if Mother Teresa had accusers, critics, detractors, and even those who considered themselves her enemies, we all are likely to have the same if we are so bold as to succeed in life. There will always be the jealous, unfair, negative people who will do their best to prevent others from succeeding in life; succeed anyway. After all, it was never about these people, it was about you and your goals and dreams.

Final Thoughts

You may have noticed that I took my own advice over the chapters of this book. I started with a heavy emphasis on the trauma that can alter the course of an individual's life. But as the book progressed there was less and less emphasis on trauma because my advice is to do the same in your life. Healing is very important, but it is a stop along the journey of life and not a place to get so used to that you reside there. It is not that I believe trauma ever goes away — this only occurs with memory loss or dissociation, both symptoms of a disorder. Healthy people remember the bad things that have happened in their lives but they work to not let negative events dominate their memories, their feelings or their potential for the future.

I will have failed in this book if you have read to this point and said either, "That was interesting," or "That was a waste of time." I will have succeeded if you have reached this point, and you have: first, realized the extent of influence you have over your life and your experience of it; second, identified several places where you want to make improvements in this life you are producing and you are directing; and finally, already begun to make your life more harmonious with your beliefs, your dreams, and your potential. Trauma tempts everyone it touches to build their lives around negativity and limitations. Do not give your potential away to trauma without putting up a fight, and, let's be real, it may be the fight of your life. But this is exactly the point of this book: to move from healing to reaching your potential and your goals is the fight of and for your life. It is well worth the effort and struggle to give your dreams all the energy you have within you in order to arrive at what is the ultimate destination: personal contentment.

THE PATH TO PERSONAL CONTENTMENT

Make sure you do the healing yourself.

Do not stay at the healing phase of life longer than you need to.

Understand and practice the true keys to happiness.

Learn how to bounce back from adversity.

Practice bringing more positive ideas, emotions and behavior into your day.

Invest in improving your physical health.

Build a strong social support network and put time and energy into giving and receiving support.

Make an effort to live according to your beliefs, one decision at a time.

Personal contentment does not come

REFERENCES

Alsbury, C. & Alsbury, G. (2003). *Consciousness.* Alsbury Films.

Arntz, W., Chasse, B. & Hoffman, M. (2004). *What The Bleep Do We Know?* Captured Light & Lord of the Winds Films. Beverly Hills: Twentieth Century Fox.

Aspinwall, L.G. & Leaf, S.L. (2002). In search of the unique aspects of hope: Pinning our hopes on positive emotions, future-oriented thinking, hard times, and other people. *Psychological Inquiry, 13*, 276-288.

Bacharowski. J.A., & Owen, M.J. (2001). Not all laughs are alike: voiced but not unvoiced laughter readily elicits positive affect. *Psychological Science, 12(3)*, 252-257.

Baker, D. & Stauth, C. (2002). *What Happy People Know: How the new science of happiness can change your life for the better.* Rodale Press.

Berk, L., Felten, D., Tan, S., Bittman, & Westengard, J. (2001). Modulation of neuroimmune parameters during the eustress of humor-associated mirthful laughter. *Alternative Therapy Health Medicine 7,* 62-72.

Boehm, J.K. & Lyubomirsky, S. (in press). Enduring happiness. In S. J. Lopez (Eds.) *Handbook of Positive Psychology.* Oxford: Oxford University Press.

Bowlby, J. (1982). *Attachment.* New York: Basic Books.

Byrne, R. (2007). *The Secret.* New York: Simon & Schuster and Beyond Words Publishing.

Carver, C.S. & Scheier, M.F. (2005). Engagement, disengagement, coping, and catastrophe. In: A. Elliot, C. Dweck (Eds), *Handbook of Competence and Motivation.* New York: Guilford. 527-547.

Cousins, N. (1979). *Anatomy of an illness as perceived by the patient.* Toronto: Bantam Books.

Danner, D.D., Snowdon, D. A., & Friesen, W.V. (2001). Positive emotions in early life and longevity: findings from the nun study. *Personality Processes and Individual Differences, 80*(5), 804-813.

Davidson, R.J. (2004). Well-being and affective style: neural substrates and biobehavioral correlates. *Phil. Trans. R. Soc. London, B359*, 1395-1411.

Diener, E. (2000). Explaining differences in societal levels of happiness: Relative standards, need fulfillment, culture and evaluation theory. *Journal of Happiness Studies, 1*(1), 41-78.

Diener, E., & Diener, C. (1995). Cross-cultural correlates of life satisfaction and self-satisfaction and self-esteem. *Journal of Personality and Social Psychology, 68*, 653-663.

Easterbrook, G. (2003) *The Progress Paradox*. New York: Random House.

Exline, J.J., Yali, A.M. & Sanderson, W.C. (2000). Guilt, discord, and alienation: The role of religious strain in depression suicidality. *Journal of Clinical Psychology, 56*, 1481-1496.

Felitti, V.J., Anda, R.F., Nordenberg, D., Williamson, D.F., Spitz, A.M., Edwards, V., & Koss, M.P. (1998). The relationship of adult health status to childhood abuse and household dysfunction. *American Journal of Preventive Medicine, 14*, 245-258.

Fulghum, R. (1989). *All I Really Need to Know I Learned In Kindergarten*. New York: Ballantine Publishing.

Fredickson, B.L. (2004). Gratitude, like other positive emotions, broadens and builds. In R.A. Emmons & M.E. McCullough, (Eds.). *The Psychology of Gratitude*. New York: Oxford University Press.

Goswani, A. (2004). In Arntz, W., Chasse, B. & Hoffman, M. (2004). *What The Bleep Do We Know?"* Captured Light & Lord of the Winds Films. Beverly Hills: Twentieth Century Fox.

Hallowell, E.M. *The Childhood Roots Of Adult Happiness.* (2002). New York: Ballantine Books.

Hameroff, S. (2003). In *Consciousness*. Alsbury Films.

Harris, A.H. & Thoresen, C.E. (2005). Forgiveness, unforgiveness, health and disease. In E.L. Worthington Jr. (Ed.), *Handbook of Forgiveness*. New York: Brunner-Routledge.

Harris, A.H., Thoresen, C.E. & Lopez, S.J. (2007). Integrating Positive Psychology Into Counseling: Why and (When Appropriate) How. *Journal of Counseling & Development, 85*(1), 3-13.

Helliwell, J. & Putnam, R.D. (2004). The social context of well-being. In F.A. Huppert, B. Keverne & N. Baylis, (Eds.). *The Science of Well-being.* Oxford: Oxford University Press.

House, J.S., Landis, K.R. & Umberson D. (1988). Social relationships and health. *Science 241*, 540-545.

Huppert, F.A. & Whittington, J.E. (1995). Symptoms of psychological distress predict seven-year mortality. *Psychological Medicine, 25*, 1073-1086.

Huther, G. (2006). *The Compassionate Brain, how empathy creates intelligence.* Boston: Trumpeter Press.

Judge, T.A., Toresen, C.J., Bono, J.E. & Patton, G.K. (2001). The job satisfaction-job performance relationship: a qualitative and quantitative review. *Psychological Bulletin, 127*(3), 376-407.

Kubzansky, L.D. & Kawachi, I. (2000). Going to the heart of the matter. Negative emotions and coronary heart disease. *Psychosomatic Research, 48*, 323-337.

Kubzansky, L.D., Sparrow, D., Vokonas, P. & Kawachi, I. (2001). Is the glass half empty or half full? A prospective study of optimism and coronary heart disease in the normative aging study. *Psychosomatic Medicine, 63*, 910-916.

Lyubomirsky, S., King, L. & Diener, E. (2006). The benefits of frequent positive affect: Does happiness lead to success? *Psychological Bulletin, 131*, 803-855.

Mahony, D.L., Burroughs, W.J. & Hieatt, A.C. (2001). The effects of laughter on discomfort thresholds: Does expectation become reality: *Journal of General Psychology, 128*(2), 217-226.

Marieb, E.N. (1995). *Human Anatomy and Physiology.* New York: Benjamin/Cummings.

Maslow, A. (1970). *Motivation & Personality.* New York: Harper & Row.

McCullough, M.E., Hoyt, W.T., Larson D.B., Koenig, H.G. & Thoresen, C.E. (2000). Religious involvement and mortality: A meta-analytic review. *Health Psychology, 19*, 211-222.

McCullough, M.E., Pargament, K.I., & Thoresen, C.E. (Eds.). (2000). *Forgiveness: Theory, research, and practice.* New York: Guilford Press.

McEwen, B.S. (1998). Protective and damaging effects of stress mediators. *New England Journal of Medicine, 338*, 171-179.

Middleton, R.A. & Byrd, E.K. (1996). Psychosocial factors and hospital readmission status of older persons with cardiovascular disease. *Journal of Applied Rehabilitation Counseling, 27*, 3-10.

Moore, T. (1992). *Care of the Soul, A Guide for Cultivating Depth and Sacredness in Everyday Life.* New York: Harper Collins.

Neborsky, R.J. (2003). A clinical model for the comprehensive treatment of trauma using an affect experiencing-attachment theory approach. In *Healing Trauma*, New York: W.W. Norton & Company.

Ornish, D. (1990). Can lifestyle changes reverse coronary heart disease? The lifestyle heart trial. *Lancet 336*(8708), 129-133.

Pennebaker, J.W., Kiecolt-Glaser, J.K. & Glaser, R. (1988). Disclosure of traumas and immune function: Health implications for psychotherapy. *Journal of Consulting and Clinical Psychology, 56*(2), 239-245.

Perry, B.D. (1994). Neurobiological sequelae of childhood trauma: Post-traumatic stress disorders in children. In M. Murberg (Ed.), *Catecholamines in post-traumatic stress disorder emerging concepts.* Washington, DC: American Psychiatric Press.

Ratey, J.J. (2001). *A User's Guide To The Brain.* New York: Vintage Books.

Ratey, J.J. (2007). *Spark: The Revolutionary New Science of Exercise and the Brain.* New York: Little, Brown & Company.

Ryan, R.M. & Deci, E.L. (2001). On happiness and human potentials: A review of research on hedonic and eudaimonic well-being. *Annual Reviews of Psychology,* *52,* 141-166.

Seligman, M. (2002). *Authentic Happiness: Using the New Positive Psychology to Realize Your Potential for Lasting Fulfillment.* New York: The Free Press.

Seligman, M. (1998). *Learned Optimism: How to Change Your Mind and Your Life.* New York: Nippon.

Selye, H. (1946). The general adaptation syndrome and the diseases of adaptation. *Journal of Clinical Endocrinology Metab.* 6, 117-230.

Siegel, D.J. (2003). An interpersonal neurobiology of psychotherapy. In *Healing Trauma.* New York: W.W. Norton & Company.

Sloan, R.P., Bagiella, E. & Powell, T. (2001). Without a prayer: methodological problems, ethical challenges, and misrepresentations with the study of religion, spirituality, and medicine. In T.G. Plante & A.C. Sherman (Eds.), *Faith and Health.* New York: Guilford Press.

Solomon, M.F. & Siegel, D.J. (2003). *Healing Trauma.* New York: W.W. Norton & Company.

Wallechinsky, D. (2007). "Where America Leads the World." *Parade.* New York: Parade Publications.

Webster's *Encyclopedic Unabridged Dictionary of the English Language.* (2001). New York: Thunder Bay Press.

Wolf, F.A. (1989). *Taking the Quantum Leap: The New Physics for Nonscientists.* New York: Harper & Row.

Woolf, N.J. (2003). In Alsbury, C. & Alsbury, G. (2003). *Consciousness.* Alsbury Films.

Ziegler, D.L. (2000). *Raising Children Who Refuse To Be Raised, Parenting Skills and Therapy Interventions For The Most Difficult Children.* Phoenix: Acacia Publishing.

Ziegler, D.L. (2002). *Traumatic Experience And The Brain, A Handbook For Understanding And Treating Those Traumatized As Children.* Phoenix: Acacia Publishing.

Dave Ziegler

Ziegler, D.L. (2005). *Achieving Success With Impossible Children, How To Win The Battle Of Wills.* Phoenix: Acacia Publishing.
Ziegler, D.L. (2006). *The Attachment Disorder Assessment Scale – Revised Manual.* Phoenix: Acacia Publishing.

Also from the author of
Beyond Healing

Raising difficult children can be a daunting task, but Dr. Dave Ziegler can help. *Raising Children who Refuse to Be Raised* (2000) deals with problems ranging from ADHD to attachment issues, from manipulation to deeply antisocial behavior.

"If you are a parent or therapist of a child who lies, steals, is hyperactive, traumatized, distrustful, aggressive, belligerent, or explosive, you will find in this book the fundamentals of parenting such a child. Dr. Ziegler looks at traditional understandings of children with a critical fresh eye."

– Janine Gordon, M.D., Board Certified Child & Adolescent Psychiatrist

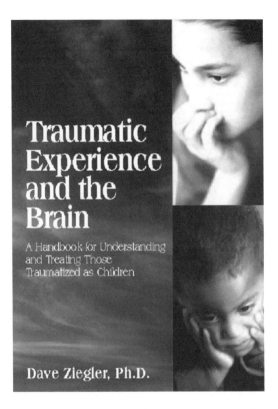

Traumatic
Experience
and the
Brain

A Handbook for Understanding
and Treating Those
Traumatized as Children

Dave Ziegler, Ph.D.

Some of us wish for our childhood to go on and on. Others, however, wish it would finally end. *Traumatic Experience and the Brain* (2002) describes how trauma experienced early in life physically affects the brain, actually rewiring one's perceptions of and reactions to self, others, and the world. The book vividly describes how, with love, therapy, and support, parents and therapists of these "broken" children can help them to overcome their past experiences and lead normal adult lives.

"Ziegler melds together years of clinical experience in treating severely traumatized children with an up-to-date understanding of how trauma affects the brain. This valuable book will help therapists and professionals recognize how the traumatized brain produces trauma symptoms and how best to intervene."

—David V. Baldwin, Ph.D., Author/Editor, Trauma Information Pages

ISBN 0-9671187-5-1; 172 pages; $19.95 + shipping and handling
To order, call Acacia Publishing toll-free: 866-265-4553

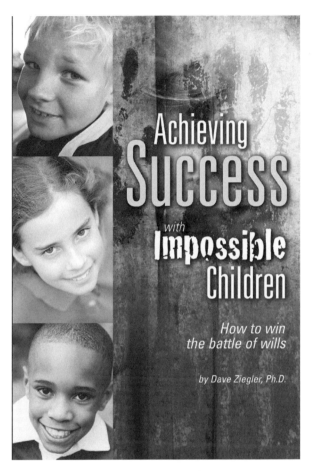

Clearly written and infused with humor, *Achieving Success* discusses working with difficult children in multiple settings such as during adoption, in school, with parents, and in residential care, offering practical applications and hands-on suggestions and stressing the importance of hope in dealing with these special children.

"Dave takes you from Parenting 101 to Graduate School. He makes the hardest principles understandable."

– D.V., Adoptive Parent

ISBN 0-9666572-9-2; 370 pages; $24.95 + shipping and handling
To order, call Acacia Publishing toll-free: 866-265-4553

Attachment Disorder Assessment Scale - Revised

Designed by Dave Ziegler and used successfully in his treatment centers for 17 years, the ADAS-R finally fills a long-unaddressed need in psychological evaluation. It is an invaluable tool for quickly and easily obtaining a reliable level of attachment concern for a young person. The scale can be easily administered in less than 15 minutes and requires no special training. The kit includes a manual, 25 score sheets, and a hard plastic carrier case.

$49.95 + shipping and handling. Additional sets of 25 score sheets are $24.95 + shipping and handling.
To order, call Acacia Publishing toll-free: 866-265-4553